Vital Conversations

"At last a book that delivers on its promises. I have found the approach, mindset and skills here invaluable for creating stronger relationships and enhancing leadership excellence. If you want more transparency, integrity and accountability in your conversations then I strongly recommend this book."
Peter Collyer, Vice President of Global Human Resources, Disney

"It is so easy to see myself (and others!) in so many of the situations Alec describes… but what is really excellent about this book is the practical, doable behaviour changing solutions. I wish I'd read the book before my first job, before my first marriage, before my first child… fortunately, it's not too late, even now!"
Ipe Jacob, Senior Partner Financial Markets Group, Grant Thornton

"In an era where leadership needs to be more humble, we also need to be honest with those around us. Alec's book is a fantastic manual to help people do the right thing, the hard thing, the difficult thing."
Aaron McCormack, CEO, BT Conferencing

"In today's current economic climate, business survival will depend heavily on a leader's willingness to face up to reality and engage others in difficult conversations that will either make or break the company's future. If you're serious about your own development, your key relationships and your company's success then make this book a priority."
Graham Kingsmill, CEO Maxima and former CEO, SAP UK

"I have over the years been asked to review several business books. Quite frankly most of them are as boring as cold toast! Alec's book is thankfully not one of those. I found when I started reading it I didn't want to stop. I learnt things I frankly should have known, and am ashamed of getting wrong for so long, simple but effective techniques. I heartily recommend it."
Jo Haigh, Head of Corporate Finance, MGR and author of Tales from the Glass Ceiling, A Survival Guide for Women in Business

"The ability to step up and successfully engage in a vital conversation is a key attribute of an effective leader and yet surprisingly, this skill set is usually absent from leadership development programmes. My research into emerging leadership paradigms reveals that this aspect of communication skills is crucial for success in today's complex business environments. Alec's approach to raising tough issues with transparency, integrity and respect is both refreshing and inspiring."
Vlatka Hlupic, Professor of Business and Management, Westminster Business School

"What are the most critical incidents which have shaped you as a leader? This book is an invaluable resource to aid your ability to undertake those defining conversations that can either make or break a team, relationship or key project. I recommend it highly."
Megan Reitz, Client & Programme Director, Ashridge Business School

"At last, a robust yet accessible book that guides you like a SATNAV through the complexities of your most difficult conversations."
Jan Bloomfield, Executive Director of Workforce & Communications, West Suffolk Hospital

"A rich and valuable resource... Alec Grimsley offers his readers the insights, the tools, and the courage to tackle their most dreaded, stomach-churning conversations. Best of all, his highly ethical approach lights the way to honest dialogue and genuine understanding."
Adele Faber, co-author of How to Talk So Kids Will Listen & Listen So Kids Will Talk and Siblings Without Rivalry

"What is left unsaid often causes more problems than what is said. This book takes the fear out of those difficult conversations we'd all rather avoid. It's clear, well organised and, above all, totally practical, with strategies that can transform your business and personal life."
Jurgen Wolff, author of Successful Scriptwriting and Your Writing Coach

"Alec Grimsley has provided an invaluable addition to the difficult/vital conversation arena. If you read one self development book this year make sure it's this one!"
Malcolm Stern, Channel 4 presenter, psychotherapist and specialist in conflict resolution

"This book is largely common sense, but a kind of common sense that is rare. When faced with the need to have, or during, a vital conversation, most of us are beset with a variety of strong emotions, and then our good sense flies out of the window. This book illustrates many situations with clear examples from home and work life, and walks the reader through a series of approaches and preparatory processes that should make our vital conversations far less daunting and more rewarding – for both parties. A vital read!"
Sir John Whitmore, author of Coaching for Performance and Chair of Performance Consultants International

"An essential read for any CEO who must have that conversation to make the impossible possible."
Chris Bown, Chief Executive, West Suffolk Hospital NHS Trust

Vital Conversations

Making the
impossible conversation
POSSIBLE

Alec Grimsley

First published by Barnes Holland Publishing Ltd in 2010

Barnes Holland Publishing Ltd
The Old Star
Church Street
Princes Risborough
HP27 9AA

ISBN: 978-0-9563128-0-8

British Library Cataloguing in Publication Data
A catalogue record for this book is available from the
British Library.

Printed in the UK.

Contents

Acknowledgements

This is my first book and I think I've made every mistake there was to make as a first-time author. As with nearly all great endeavours, they are rarely achieved without support, so I would like to offer my sincere thanks and appreciation to the following people.

First to my wife Gill, whose love, support and challenge have kept me sane and this book on track. It is Gill who witnessed my highs and lows, including my struggle and guilt to balance running a business, writing a book and being a father and husband.

My editor Sally Lansdell has been amazing: her feedback and talent for shaping structure and content have made all the difference.

A big thank-you to Symon, Meg, Mary, Daniel, Chris and Malcolm, who all gave their time to read and critique the book: your help was greatly appreciated. I would also like to thank all those people who agreed to be interviewed around life experiences that benefited from or could have benefited from a vital conversation. Your openness helped to bring this book alive.

A big thank-you to my mum and dad, who have always shown me what creativity, determination and hard work can produce.

Finally thank you Joshua, my young son, whose love, hugs and laughter helped to raise my spirits on many a "bad" writing day. Although I'm not sure his feedback that the book needed far more giants, aliens, boats and songs was that helpful!

Prologue

"Our lives begin to end the day we become silent about things that matter most."
                                        Martin Luther King

How many conversations have you had in the last twelve months? Adults have over 10,000 conversations a year, from chatting with family and friends to meetings with peers and clients. Even the everyday "life stuff" like shopping and booking a restaurant requires two-way dialogue.

Out of all those conversations, only a tiny fraction will be what I would term vital. If you look in the dictionary you will see that vital means "necessary for the continuation of life" or "urgently needed and absolutely crucial". In essence, vital conversations are just that: must-have conversations that will help to move your business, teams and key personal relationships forward. They are the most important conversations you will ever have.

But there's a dilemma. You know deep down that there are issues to be resolved or words and feelings that must be expressed, and you sense that this one conversation could make a real difference. Unfortunately, you may also feel overwhelmed by strong emotions or fearful of how the conversation may play out. It's no wonder that many people stay silent about the things that matter to them most.

To quote Ken Blanchard, "While no single conversation is guaranteed to change the trajectory of a career, a business, a marriage, or a life, any single conversation can." This book looks at how to identify and then successfully engage in the conversations that will make the biggest difference for *you*.

Confront or avoid?

I always advise those I coach to check and double check their reasoning and motivations before embarking on a vital conversation. Conversations of this magnitude can be very challenging, complex and unpredictable. The other person may react badly to your point of view or you may hurt their feelings in ways that you did not intend. In some cases, once you have engaged the other person in the conversation, there is no turning back, the genie is out of the bottle, and the significance of the issues discussed may change the nature of your relationship for ever, whether the conversation goes the way you had hoped or not.

But I also coach those who seek my help to think long and hard about the consequences of *not* having the conversation. It's all too easy to let our fear or discomfort monopolise our mind and we can swiftly begin to talk ourselves out of taking action. Yet the downstream ramifications of not engaging in the right conversation can be incredibly debilitating to our career, organisation, relationships and personal happiness.

In my research in writing this book and through running workshops and facilitating senior teams, I have coached or interviewed many people who have either taken on or chosen to avoid high-stakes conversations. Several of these people have kindly given me permission to pass on their experiences to you. Let's start by taking a look at two real-life case studies and consider the impact of confronting or avoiding a vital conversation. The names and some aspects of the content have been changed to protect and respect confidentiality.

Real-life case study: Dad, we need to talk

For as long as Martin could remember he had yearned for a more meaningful relationship with his father. As a child he was afraid of him, and as an adult he had put distance between them both psychologically and geographically. Martin's visits to his parents' home were infrequent, but they often ended up in frustrating or painful arguments. His need for a closer connection was confused by powerful feelings of anger and sadness regarding the way the dynamics of their relationship had played out in the past. Martin had recently attended one of my workshops and confided in me that this was the vital conversation he was using the workshop to prepare for. A management consultant by profession, he was used to robust business conversations, but had little experience of or stomach for talking about issues so close to the heart. He shared with me his fear of the emotional minefield he would have to navigate his way through. Yet he also knew that if ever hoped to develop a more meaningful friendship with his dad, he would have to discuss the undiscussable.

Four weeks after the workshop, from a beach close to his parents' home in Cornwall and hands trembling, Martin called his father on the mobile. With a bone-dry mouth and racing heart, he asked his dad to meet him at the far end of the beach. All Martin said was that he had something important to discuss. He was expecting the usual 20-question interrogation from his dad, but on this occasion all he got back down the line was "I'll be down in 20 minutes".

Martin put the phone back in his pocket and was overcome with nausea as adrenalin coursed through his veins, and the implications of igniting this conversation suddenly became all too real. His mind was awash with challenging thoughts: "Can I stand up to my father and say what needs to be said? Will he laugh my feelings off as nonsense, creating a yet wider gulf between us? Will he put me through a guilt trip? What if he cries, do I have the right to open my father up to that level of emotional pain just because I want a better relationship?"

Using everything he had gained from the workshop and his life experiences to date, Martin tried his best to remain calm and, clinging tightly to his positive intent to develop a closer, more meaningful friendship with his father, he embarked on this highly uncertain conversation.

In Martin's words, "Initially it didn't go well. Let's face it, however carefully you choose your words, how many dads would want to hear that their son felt they had a crap relationship? I think in hindsight my dad had lower expectations about what could be hoped for in a father–son relationship, so it was hard for me to describe how I felt without it sounding to him like I saw him as a poor father. It was also hard to keep my emotions in check and my thinking clear, and at times the conversation jumped around and became confusing. But slowly, as we moved beyond hearing to listening, we began to express openly our fears and misunderstandings, and our regrets about the past, revealing the early dawn of a new relationship. In that 45-minute conversation we became closer than I can ever recall and for the first time in 28 years my father and I hugged."

Martin went on to say: "Even with my limited skills and experience, it was worth taking on this conversation. Since that day just over three years ago we must have had hundreds of conversations, many of them the everyday exchanges of 'How are you doing?' and 'What have you been up to?' And yet the authenticity, openness and respect that have developed between us have transformed our friendship. It's scary to think that if I'd remained silent back then, all of those conversations and three further years of relationship would have been contaminated by an unresolved and antagonistic past.

Real-life case study: The heavy price of ignoring your intuition

David ran a successful and growing events catering business, with turnover going beyond £10 million in just five years. He was a great salesman: he loved doing the big deals but hated the detail of looking after the financial aspects. It was obvious to him that he needed someone with real experience to manage the company finances, so he began his search for a finance director. Luckily, a close family friend who had all the right credentials was looking for a new opportunity and after an informal interview, David appointed Andrew as his finance director.

Over the next 12 months the business continued to grow, with excellent high-margin contracts. David was keen to continue the expansion and put forward plans to the finance director for further investments. When Andrew explained that the company didn't have the reserves to fund this next step, David was surprised due to the profitability of the work he'd won, but bowed to the experience of his FD, and adjusted the plans of the business to be in line with the more conservative estimates.

As each month passed, David experienced increasing unease over the profitability of the business. The financial reports he received still showed a profit, but margins were poor compared to the significant rises in turnover and incremental operational costs. David had reached a point where he wanted to challenge Andrew's running of the finances directly, but did not want create a potential rift with someone who was a close friend.

In February 2007 a brilliant opportunity arose to acquire a competitor. When David asked the finance director to arrange the funding, Andrew repeatedly missed the deadlines to have the paperwork and funding in place. Still not wishing to confront Andrew, but infuriated with his lack of progress, David simply informed him that he would be hiring an external firm of accountants to prepare the accounts and raise the financing.

Two days later, David took a phone call he will never forget. Andrew's wife, in floods of tears, was calling to share the tragic news that Andrew had taken his own life. Even before the external audit was half way completed, it became obvious that Andrew had been embezzling large amounts of money, eventually to the tune of over £1.2 million.

Although David will never know the exact reasons Andrew committed suicide, it's his belief that the inevitable prison sentence, shame and public humiliation for him and his family was too great to bear. Unfortunately, David could not pull the business back from the level of insolvency he found it in and it went under, with the loss of 78 jobs.

When David agreed to share his story in this book, he explained that in his own mind, if he'd had the courage to challenge his friend 12 months before when all his intuition was nagging him to do so, he would have still have had to fire him, their friendship would have come to an abrupt end and the police may still have prosecuted him. However, David would still have had his business and, more importantly, Andrew may well have been alive today.

Giving you the right tools and approach

These two case studies are just some of the many real-life stories that have inspired me to make it my life's purpose to help others identify and successfully engage in vital yet often very difficult conversations. As a mediator I have observed too many people who have endured an unnecessarily high level of suffering, frustration and pain because they did not have the mindset, skills or process to resolve their differences. I have invested countless days in developing, practising and honing the approach laid out in this book.

As part of my research for writing *Vital Conversations*, I read over 40 books that offered a variety of takes on handling difficult conversations. Many organised their approach based on dealing with and neutralising defined stereotypes, pigeonholing the other person with such labels as Mr Angry, guilt tripper, back stabber, gossiper, sulker and so on. To me this philosophy seems more divisive than useful, as it only serves to polarise the two parties, casting the other person as an enemy or a flawed human being. Think about it: haven't we all acted out some of those labels at some point in our lives?

Other books liken their approach to martial arts, where the objective is to redirect the other person's negative energy. This can be a neat parable, but it doesn't offer nearly enough depth to handle the complexity we find in resolving high-stakes issues. Again, I'm also not comfortable with seeing the other person as an opponent who needs to be controlled, even if the author only intends it as a metaphor.

Probably the best literature on this subject comes from those who have a great deal of experience in communication and facilitation. In particular, the work of Chris Argyris, Don Schon and Roger Schwarz puts forward a theory of letting go of the need to be right or to control the conversation. These authors advise the reader instead to shift to having "mutual learning" conversations. This type of thinking is a breath of fresh air, as the underlying assumptions stem from a belief that each person has a unique view of the world and that a significant part of arriving at a win–win outcome results from asking about and understanding how both parties see and feel about the issues involved.

Nevertheless, as useful as some of these books are, elements of the overall package are still missing. Although some of the better authors describe *why* we should have difficult conversations and eloquently describe *what* is involved, in my opinion they offer very little on *how* to have such a conversation.

In brief, my research highlighted three critical areas that have either not been addressed in other books, or not in sufficient detail to be useful:

❖ There was little or no guidance for the reader on where in their life, business or career they need to have a vital conversation. Although you may have picked up this book because you already know which vital conversation or significant issue you need to address, our lives are hectic and without help and coaching people can often remain blind to other areas where such a conversation is necessary.

❖ There were few strategies and tools for managing your emotions throughout the conversation. High-stakes conversations require people to be incredibly self-aware and emotionally resilient, and in my opinion it's not enough simply to point out that feelings are central to a vital conversation. As you will discover in this book, if you can't positively influence yourself, you have little or no chance of positively influencing the other person or the outcome.

❖ Great straplines like Stephen Covey's "Seek first to understand and then be understood" are without doubt wise and motivational. Unfortunately, without the "how to" it's like being inspired to sail across the Atlantic, only to realise 20 miles offshore that you don't know how to handle a yacht in a force 8 gale. When your vital conversation starts to capsize, you need a robust set of skills to keep it from sinking.

So why are you reading this book?

Time is precious, so if you're investing that rarest of commodities in reading this book, the chances are you're someone who cares deeply about improving the quality of your communication and your relationships. Alternatively, you may be in the darker, more ominous position of needing to make a significant change in your business or in a key relationship, and you're only too aware that any brighter future will involve at least one if not several difficult conversations.

You may also be reading this book for one of the following reasons:

❖ You know you need to have a vital conversation but you're too afraid to have it.

❖ Your job includes the requirement to have difficult conversations and you want to improve your skills and approach.

❖ Your inability to deal with conflict is holding you back and restricting your career potential.

❖ A part of your life or relationship isn't working out right now and you need to have a conversation with one or more people, but you're not sure how to go about it.

❖ For the long-term health of the business, you need to give certain people some bad news.

❖ You care very deeply about key people in your life and you want to deepen that connection by communicating in a respectful, transparent and authentic way.

❖ You have a reputation at work for being a fire-breathing dragon and the HR director has left this book on your desk while you were away from your office!

What is *your* reason?

There are no easy vital conversations

As a professional mediator, coach, husband and father, I can hand on heart tell you that whatever level of skill you believe you have, there are no easy vital conversations. If you come across literature or a guru who claims they have a blueprint that makes it easy, I recommend a healthy dose of scepticism.

I've had the honour and pleasure of working with and learning from some of the world's most talented people in the field of conflict resolution – and all of them, without exception, have found certain difficult conversations extremely challenging. So if the thought of engaging in a vital conversation terrifies you, you're in good company!

With so much of our success, happiness and peace of mind tied to the quality of our communication and cooperation with others, my experience leads me to believe that the quality of our life and relationships is dependent on the quality of our conversations. My role throughout this book is to be your mentor and coach, and to help develop your approach, skills and confidence. The book provides robust strategies for making the impossible conversation possible. If you follow my guidance and apply what this book has to offer, it will bring you to a new way of thinking and communicating, leading to enhanced relationships, better results and greater peace of mind.

I also commit to you now not to overpromise. Completely eliminating all fear and anxiety from a vital yet difficult conversation is an unrealistic goal, but minimising the fear and anxiety is definitely within our grasp. Similarly, expecting a fantastic outcome to every vital conversation is blind optimism, but a significant improvement in the outcome is consistently achievable.

Who knows? There may be just a handful of vital conversations between where you find yourself now, and where you most want your life, career or business to be!

Part I
Introduction

1

How to Get the Most from This Book

"An expert is a person who has made all the mistakes to be made in a very narrow field."

Niels Bohr, physicist and Nobel Prize winner

Imagine asking someone who's never been to London to drive to an address in the central business district with no map or GPS. Not only would they frequently get lost and therefore frustrated, it's likely they would give up easily or even be too overwhelmed to attempt the journey in the first place.

Like navigating a major inner-city road network, both vital conversations and the people involved in them can be complex and unpredictable. I offer this book and my experience as your personal satellite navigation system, helping you plan a route to a successful conversational destination. Like a top-of-the-range sat nav, I'm also here to advise you of roadblocks and danger signs, offering you the skills to reverse out of verbal cul-de-sacs and the resilience to handle the strong emotions of a person who's experiencing the conversational equivalent of road rage!

I start by offering a verbal map of how this book is organised to support your learning and progress. Each chapter is designed to help you to break down even your most difficult conversations into manageable chunks, increasing your belief and motivation to create a successful outcome.

Why we all avoid vital conversations

Everyone procrastinates over things they find difficult, including conversations. Chapter 2 explains why and helps you face up to the costs of doing so, as well as outlining the essential elements of a vital conversation.

Your vital conversations audit

You will get more value from this book if you connect the learning to actual conversations that you need to have. Knowledge is rarely transformed into personal wisdom unless you apply what you learn to the real world. If you use one of your own examples, the book comes to life as your vital conversations coach. Use Chapter 3 to highlight which conversations you want to have in both your personal and your professional life.

Foundational mindsets

"Who you are speaks so loudly, I cannot hear what you are saying."

Ralph Waldo Emerson

Chapter 4 explores three levels or "generations" of thinking that people either consciously choose or habitually fall into during a vital conversation:

❖ First-generation thinking is the fight/flight response, a knee-jerk reaction to a real or perceived threat, including a difficult conversation that feels psychologically unsafe. Unfortunately, this is still many people's predominant mindset, leading to either hostility or docility in their vital conversations.

❖ Second-generation thinking has "command and control" at its core. It has evolved from first-generation thinking to include a cleverly disguised veneer of interpersonal skills. From this mindset you can achieve win/lose, short-term results by manipulating the other person to your way of thinking. I will address why this level of thinking is so prolific at both work and home, as well as the long-term consequences for relationships that come from this frame of reference, including the erosion of trust and an increase in scepticism and resistance.

❖ Third-generation thinking represents a new level of consciousness. It demands that you significantly raise the bar mentally and begin to see your interactions as "mutual understanding conversations". In this mental space you are no longer motivated by a mindset of winning or losing or right versus wrong, but instead you allow your approach to be guided by underlying values such as compassion, courage, curiosity and collaboration. When the conversation is vital and challenging, these underlying values become your compass. They don't guarantee a successful outcome, but they do give you a fighting chance of staying resourceful, looking after the relationship, and finding a productive way forward.

Mastering your emotional state

"Let's not forget that the little emotions are the great captains of our lives and we obey them without realising it."

Vincent Van Gogh

If you build a new house on unstable ground, then at some point you're likely to encounter major structural problems. In the same way, the foundation of an effective vital conversation is your ability to start from a secure emotional footing.

Have you ever experienced the following situation? You're feeling really angry about someone's behaviour or a decision they've made, and that person is in close proximity to you. Even though you know that what you would like to say will probably hurt the relationship and not solve anything, you seem powerless to stop yourself and in the blink of an eye you've blurted something out that you later regret. To cap it all, you were the one that was negatively affected by this person's actions, and now due to your outburst you're the one who ends up apologising!

In essence, you can either have your emotions or they are going to have you. With increased self-awareness and some practical tools, you can begin to gain far more control over your emotional state and subsequently behave more effectively in your conversations with other people.

In Chapters 5–8, having explained how the mind and body can combine to generate powerful feelings, I share strategies and tools for recognising the signs that you are becoming emotionally charged. Rather than switching off from your emotions, going neutral or numbing out, I explain how to cultivate the skill of observing and acknowledging strong feelings.

Once you can go beyond denying or suppressing your feelings, you can:

❖ Choose not to act on these powerful emotions.
❖ Generate different and more resourceful emotions like curiosity, courage and compassion.
❖ Share with other people how you are feeling in a safe and respectful way.

Understanding and preparing for a vital conversation

"One of life's most painful moments comes when we must admit that we didn't do our homework, that we were not prepared."
Merlin Olsen

In Chapter 9 the book coaches you through a pragmatic approach to preparing for a vital conversation. The concepts and coaching tools will enable you metaphorically to go to higher ground, gaining a broader, more rational perspective on the issues and people involved and increasing your confidence to engage in the conversation ahead. Crucially, you will discover how to question and reassess your perceptions of the issues and people involved.

From the mini case study below you can see that Gareth's words and approach to the conversation are being heavily influenced by his perceptions or "mental story" as I call it (annotated in the left-hand column).

Unlike Gareth, you will gain insights into taking control of your own mental storytelling, becoming ruthlessly honest with yourself about its accuracy and validity. Unfortunately, through a combination of being unconsciously controlled by his perceptions, unchecked emotions and a lack of preparation, Gareth's kneejerk conversation was doomed from the start, and now not only does he have a strained relationship with Elizabeth, he's probably derailed any chances of getting his new product proposals back on the table any time soon.

You can also see how Gareth has cast Liz as someone with dubious motives. In this section of the book I will also raise your awareness around how quickly both parties can inaccurately assume negative intentions due to the impact of the other person's behaviour and actions. Furthermore, if you are able to be brutally honest with yourself, you will gain significant insights into how you may have contributed to the issues you want to discuss.

Gareth, the marketing director, is walking to Elizabeth's office. Elizabeth is the manufacturing director. Twenty minutes earlier, Gareth was facing a barrage of searching questions from Elizabeth in the weekly senior management team meeting. Her questions raised doubts in the CEO's mind about Gareth's plans for a new product line and the CEO all but killed the possibility of taking this innovative product to market by asking Gareth to "Put in on the back burner for the time being", which was an indirect way of saying forget it! Gareth is angry with Elizabeth, because in his mind Elizabeth's aggressive questioning was just not necessary, given that the product was still at the concept stage. He is a firm believer that the future success of this company needs to come from fostering innovative ideas rather than killing concepts even before they have had a chance to be proven. Gareth also has a story in his head that Elizabeth, who's been in her position for 10 years, just wants an easy life and doesn't want the headache of considering new production processes and factory layouts, and that it's in her own interests to kill off initiatives like this before they can gain any momentum.

Here is the conversation, in which I have added what Gareth is thinking but not actually saying.

What Gareth was thinking and feeling but didn't say	What they actually said to each other
	GARETH: Hey Elizabeth, I need to talk to you about what happened in the meeting.
	ELIZABETH: Sure, but it'll need to be quick.
GARETH: I see. Now you're conveniently in a rush. You probably thought you'd get away with your SS interrogation style and now you don't want to have a difficult conversation with me.	GARETH: Let me get straight to the point. Was it really necessary to undermine my ideas on the new product line?
	ELIZABETH: I'm not sure what you're getting at.
GARETH: Don't try and play the innocent with me.	GARETH: You know exactly what I mean, Liz. You killed off this project before it even had a chance of being proven a winner. Why do you have to be so defensive to new ideas?
	ELIZABETH: Look Gareth, I have 10 years' experience and I'm paid to make sure this company can actually produce and deliver on its promises to the customer. I only asked the questions that any half-decent manufacturing director should. If you struggled to come up with the answers to satisfy the board, then don't blame me for your lack of preparation.
GARETH: Typical Liz, playing the paid to be pessimistic card, to hide your real agenda around not having to change things.	GARETH: Come on Liz, be honest with me, you just saw this new product line as a bunch of extra work you don't need.
	ELIZABETH: I have people waiting outside for a meeting, so if you're insinuating I placed personal reasons ahead of the company's best interests, I think this is a conversation we'd better have with the MD and the HR director present. So if you want to accuse me of dubious intent, please talk to my PA and arrange a meeting. I have nothing more to say on the matter.

In Chapter 10 the book will conclude your preparation by unpacking the conversational dynamics of what will actually occur between you and the other person once engaged in dialogue. Gaining insights into the make-up of a vital conversation and also reconnecting to the spirit of the third-generation approach is a perfect foundation from which to apply your new-found conversational skills.

Mastering the conversation itself

Because vital conversations can involve high stakes, powerful emotions, differing opinions and even a sprinkling of historical baggage, they are likely to contain a significant degree of unpredictability. Just when you're thinking "This is going quite well", something is said that is a negative trigger to either you or the other person. The conversation now faces a real possibility of going into an irreversible downward spiral.

Rather than a vital conversation being a linear, step-by-step process, it's more akin to a game of snakes and ladders. Just like in the game, you want to reach a successful end point, but if you hit a conversational roadblock, it's like landing on a snake and the conversation takes several steps backwards. Conversely, sometimes you see eye to eye or clear up a misunderstanding and shoot up a ladder, creating a breakthrough moment in your dialogue.

Even with good preparation, many conversations never recover from a poor opening. You may be so nervous that you take an eternity to name the issue, or you may follow a steam train approach that delivers "the problem" so hard that the other party emotionally shuts down before the conversation has had a chance to get started.

You also need the inner resilience and conversational dexterity to be respectful with someone who hasn't responded well to your best efforts at kicking off the conversation. In the face of high stakes or differing opinions, it is easy for the other person to become angry, sad or generally overwhelmed. When this occurs you need to know how to pace and acknowledge these strong emotions, giving you the best possible chance of keeping a productive conversation alive.

This part of the book primarily focuses on the skills you need to maintain a respectful and productive dialogue. You will become more aware of how the approach you take and the words you use can hurt or heal relationships. I invite you to familiarise yourself with new ways of talking, which can dramatically increase the chances of creating collaboration and in many cases a mutually beneficial outcome.

There will also be times when the other person may be using words or making assumptions, accusations or comments that are very difficult to hear or accept. This is where you need techniques for remaining calm and centred. I explain skills that enable you to clarify and challenge the other person's words and thinking while maintaining rapport and productive two-way communication.

As your vital conversation progresses, it is critical to develop a shared understanding of the other person's perceptions, concerns, feelings and needs. Chapters 11 and 12 highlight how you can achieve this and then build on the mutual understanding to craft potential solutions, agreements and, if required, clearly defined next steps. Chapter 13 discusses the tricky subject of ending the conversation, and Chapter 14 is devoted specifically to when you have to give another person bad news.

Helping you navigate this book

This book incorporates the latest thinking on accelerated learning. You will get the most from it if you, most importantly, apply what you read to real vital conversations that you need to have. The following icons indicate important points.

Coaching tool

The coaching tool gets you ready for engaging in your vital conversation. You can either use the one at the back of the book (page 23) or go to my website, www.alecgrimsley.co.uk/coachingtool, and download the document to your computer using pass code mentoringtool1. The coaching tool helps you view the conversation you want to have in its entirety so that you can prepare effectively.

At various points in the book, indicated by the coaching tool icon, you will be prompted to return to the coaching tool to get ready for the next part of your vital conversation.

Key learns

Throughout the book you will see the key learn icon. These soundbites are small enough to keep at the forefront of your mind, and help remind you of some of the fundamental learning that underpins my approach.

Mini exercise

At some points I ask you to take five minutes away from your reading to reflect on or practise a particular aspect of the learning, indicated by the exercise icon.

Case study/real-life case study

A book can never replace the skill-building practice or two-way feedback offered by a workshop, but I have made every effort to provide detailed examples that show you how to apply the learning in this book to your vital conversations. From my experiences as a mediator and facilitator of conflict, I have created case studies based on real-life conversations to illustrate key concepts and common mistakes in high-pressure conversations.

I have also interviewed people who have agreed to share their stories about challenging episodes in their life and their experience of having or procrastinating over vital conversations. Their names and some elements of the case studies have been changed to maintain confidentiality.

Top tips
This icon indicates useful hints and tips to add to your toolkit for conversational effectiveness.

Warning
This icon lets you know about potential pitfalls or big conversational no-nos.

To begin the journey, I first want to take a look at why we all avoid vital conversations.

2
Why We All Avoid Vital Conversations

"How soon 'not now' becomes never."

Martin Luther, German priest

You probably like to think of yourself as honest, open and transparent. Then again, do you really want to tackle the boisterous work colleague who dominates air time at meetings? Can you bear the unease of potentially derailing yet another holiday with your spouse by raising that sensitive issue? Isn't it just easier to let it go and keep the peace?

Missing the moon

According to space expert Dave Woods, if you were to aim a rocket at the moon but your aim was 1 degree off, you would find your spacecraft missing its lunar target by 1,978 miles, a pretty big miss by anyone's standards. It's a similar story when you procrastinate over a vital conversation: that can be a significant factor in determining the ultimate destination of a business project, relationship or key life goal.

A vital conversation is like a fork in the road. In your heart of hearts you know what needs to be said and having the conversation is your best shot at taking the direction that's most likely to benefit you, the project or some wider goal. When you procrastinate, you run the risk of taking the other fork. A week later you're heading down a path that feels further and further away from what's right or useful and you're often increasingly frustrated.

Weeks or months later, you find yourself many miles from where you want to be. How did you get so far off track?

Real-life case study

Dina and Toby had recently found out they were expecting their second child approximately five years after their first. They quickly came to the realisation that the home they were living in would not easily take another child without building an extension. There was another reason for wanting to move. Toby's mother Sheila lived only a couple of streets away and she visited frequently to give Dina a hand with the chores and look after their son David. In the first year Dina and Toby were very grateful for this help, but as time moved on and Dina became more confident and competent with David, she became increasingly frustrated with her mother-in-law's views about how David should be raised. Sheila would also make negative comments about Dina's parenting skills to Toby without talking to Dina first.

So Toby and Dina told Sheila that they were planning to move around 20 miles away, to an area that was both good for primary schools and close to Toby's place of work. Instead of the negative reaction they were expecting, Sheila said, "What a great idea, I can see you'll need a much bigger house. In fact, I've been wanting to talk to you about an idea that might be great for all of us." She went on to explain that she was thinking of selling her house as it was too big for her since Toby's father had died. Wouldn't it be a great idea if they combined their financial resources to find a place together? Sheila spoke for a good 15 minutes, explaining the many advantages of a live-in grandmother. Dina was in shock and Toby didn't know how to respond, so the fact that they didn't say no became a vague yes to Sheila's proposal.

Although Dina was horrified at the thought of her escape route turning into a life sentence, Toby was the oldest of Sheila's children and believed that he should take the most responsibility in making sure his mother was OK. Toby and Dina definitely didn't want Sheila to live with them, but neither could face the turmoil and guilt that a transparent conversation of this nature might bring. The thought of having the conversation seemed more painful than the long-term consequences of letting the issue slide.

As a result, they avoided the conversation and within two weeks Sheila had sold her house for the full asking price. As each week came and went, it became harder and harder to reverse out of the situation. Six months later they were all living together in a very nice home with an annexe on the side for Sheila. Little David was over the moon that Grandma lived only a wall away and Toby was going through a period of self-justification to get straight in his mind the crazy situation he found himself in.

As for Dina, over the next two years she became more and more depressed about the situation. Her relationship with Sheila grew more polarised and eventually Dina took a part-time job just to get away from the house. This created a huge amount of guilt and internal conflict for her, as it meant that Sheila played a bigger role in raising David and Megan, the new baby, and Dina felt that her need for space was compromising her relationship with her children. Unfortunately, another consequence was an increasingly strained relationship between Dina and Toby. Toby was stuck between his mother and his wife, who in his words were bitching about each other, and he was numbly accepting of the situation.

Three years after the move came the straw that broke the camel's back. Sheila made a low-level dig and Dina exploded. In just five minutes she directed three pent-up years of anger and bitterness at her mother-in-law. After such a painful exchange, they no longer felt able to be in the same room together.

You might think at this stage they would have made plans for Sheila to buy a separate home, but unfortunately in those three years Sheila's health had deteriorated and Toby could not face the guilt of moving her out. Dina and Sheila did find a way to live together, but it wasn't easy and it certainly wasn't stress free. Sheila passed away three years later.

So one degree out or one vital conversation not had and you can miss the moon or end up somewhere you definitely don't want to be. It's probably easy for many people reading the true story above to say "I would have never let it get that far" and in this context maybe that's true, but in what other contexts do you avoid those must-have conversations and what price do you pay for your silence?

Here are some of the reasons you may procrastinate:

❖ You know there is a high degree of uncertainty in the situation. Opening that can of worms could lead to tears, silence or a more fundamental issue that's even harder to talk about.

❖ You are aware that these conversations do not always solve the issue in one hit and that you may need more time to resolve it, creating ongoing anxiety between the conversations.

❖ You have long-held beliefs that conflict and disagreement are not psychologically or physically safe.

❖ You find conversations like this overwhelming, so you may become defensive and say things you don't really mean.
❖ You struggle with knowing how to begin this type of conversation and often find yourself skirting around the key issues.
❖ You hate the levels of anxiety these confrontations invoke and you feel emotionally drained after a conversation of this nature.

The costs of avoiding vital conversations

From a business perspective, the costs of avoiding difficult conversations can be simply gigantic, both financially and in terms of team morale. Consider some research conducted in large corporations. This examined why so many company projects either significantly underperform or fail completely. Based on interviews with thousands of employees from over 100 major organisations, the feedback is startling:

❖ Nearly one third of employees described current projects they were working on as slow-motion train wrecks.
❖ Three quarters of those said that challenging the key decision maker was impossible.
❖ 40% of those said that the project was salvageable, but only 10% felt confident enough to speak up.

In another study of major firms in the US, 40% of workers interviewed stated that their manager had allowed inappropriate behaviour to go unchallenged for over a year, while 30% claimed they had put up with the behaviour for over four years!

The key reasons that many employees remained silent was that they didn't have the confidence or skill to engage in the potentially difficult yet vital conversations that were required.

Nevertheless, my experience with over 35 FTSE 250 companies and other large organisations like the NHS tells me that the inability to have vital conversations can lead to the following consequences for a business:

❖ Ineffective performance management.
❖ Low individual and team morale because of the failure to challenge inappropriate behaviour.
❖ Lack of team solidarity at strategic meetings at board level, where untested assumptions, misunderstandings, power plays and politics can lead to poorly supported decisions.
❖ Considerable financial consequences arising from employment tribunals and payoffs.
❖ Disgruntled key personnel leave, reducing the talent pool and operational effectiveness and leading to costs to hire new talent.
❖ HR departments overwhelmed with employee issues that line mangers fail to address.
❖ Key business projects failing to deliver because team members are unwilling to challenge poor decisions.
❖ Loss of both clients' trust and business if difficult issues or bad news are not communicated early enough.

At the time of writing this book, the UK, Europe and the US are facing one of the most damaging recessions since the 1920s. In a downturn it is critical to have the ability to hold vital conversations, not for business success but for business survival.

The costs to people's personal lives are also considerable. With enough coping mechanisms like alcohol, food, shopping or work to distract you, you can almost forget there's a problem at all. But the downside to avoidance is that every day you don't address a difficult issue or behaviour:

❖ You feel a little more resentful.
❖ You may become more confused or feel a sense of hopelessness.
❖ The emotion builds, which makes it even harder to talk without getting upset.

- ❖ You don't get your needs met.
- ❖ Slowly, you mentally turn the other person into a monster.
- ❖ You explode at the smallest thing they do.
- ❖ You begin to implode and lose your self-esteem and confidence.
- ❖ You feel that the other person is further violating your boundaries and expectations.
- ❖ You become ill from the "dis-ease" of not speaking the truth about what is most important to you.
- ❖ In an extreme situation, the other person may pass away and the opportunity to mend a broken relationship is lost for ever.
- ❖ Christmas and family holidays continue to be stressful and inauthentic.
- ❖ One or both parties in the relationship numb out and the relationship is doomed to apathy or continuous compromise.

 Key learn: You might pay a heavy price for procrastinating over your vital conversation.

An Arabic saying goes, "If something happens once it's very unlikely to happen again, but if it happens twice you can be sure it will happen for a third time." If one of your key relationships or an important aspect is not working and it's been that way for a while, it's unlikely to improve on its own. I'm going to assume that if you're reading this book it's likely you've decided that you're the one who needs to bring this conversation to the table. Let's begin to take a look at what that conversation might entail.

The DNA of a vital conversation

If you were to unravel the genetic code of a vital conversation, you would find five DNA strands:

❖ High stakes with significant real or perceived consequences.
❖ Opposing viewpoints
❖ Uncertainty
❖ Historical baggage and bias.
❖ Powerful emotions.

I want to look at each of these in turn.

High stakes and potential consequences

You can broadly categorise high stakes and potential consequences into two categories:

❖ Physical/tangible: One example is an expensive and mission-critical project that's going off track and could make or break the company's future.
❖ Psychological/intangible: A good example is when a senior director becomes highly defensive after receiving very specific and accurate negative feedback around their leadership style. The feedback conflicts with how they see their own capability. To acknowledge the feedback as valid may cause this director great anxiety and uncertainty. So instead they go into denial about the credibility of the feedback.

In the case study concerning Dina, Toby and Toby's mum Sheila, the high stakes were primarily psychological. Dina's peace of mind and happiness were continually compromised, but if they had attempted to engage in the vital conversation, both Sheila and Toby's psychological identities (how they see themselves) may well have been challenged. Sheila's self-image as supportive grandmother might have been threatened if they moved without her, and she would wonder how to fill her time without the children in her day-to-day life. Toby, in his view of himself as the eldest and therefore most responsible sibling, had a strong pull to be there for his mother now his dad had passed away, and might not have been able to reconcile his guilt around his complex motives for moving home.

Opposing viewpoints

If high stakes ignite powerful emotions, then opposing viewpoints certainly stoke the fire. Differing opinions are a good thing and should be celebrated for the gold nuggets they reveal: challenging the norm, creating better solutions and developing a broader understanding of how other people see the world are just some of the benefits. However, if you approach a difference in opinion from the wrong frame of mind, you can end up fanning the emotional flames and risk derailing the conversation altogether.

Differences of opinion are usually based on different perceptions of reality. Compare differences of opinion to the process of panning for gold by hand: the actual verifiable facts are as rare as tiny fragments of this precious metal, often going unnoticed in the sand and shale of personal biases and each individual's need to be right.

Uncertainty

Because of the high stakes, differing opinions and historical baggage, these conversations are not just highly charged, they are also complex. Not only do you feel uncertain about how the conversation will play out, you may also feel very anxious about your ability to handle the potential left-field curve balls that come your way in conversations of this nature.

How do Dina and Toby respond if Sheila breaks down in tears or directs a barrage of guilt and anger their way: "How could you do this after all I've done?", "What am I supposed to do with my days now?", "David needs his grandma" or, for a really angry reaction from Dina, "But we know Dina struggles to cope on her own"?

Historical baggage and bias

Baggage acts as a magnifying glass: it amplifies the other four. Have you ever known two family members or work colleagues who can't stand each other because of previous negative encounters? Their troubled history makes it virtually impossible for them to sit in the same room, let alone discuss a sensitive issue.

Also, people don't have to experience a negative encounter with somebody else directly to carry baggage or bias. Ill feeling between religious sects and social conditioning around sexual orientation, gender, age and so on can be just as effective in biasing the perceptions we have of others.

Dina's numerous unsuccessful attempts at dropping subtle hints about Sheila's level of involvement and feedback on her parenting skills may have left Dina with the belief that Sheila is never going to approve of her, so what's the point in having a difficult conversation?

Powerful emotions

I examine powerful emotions and how to handle yours in Chapter 8 and the other person's in Chapters 10 and 12. At this stage it is enough to say that if the conversation has become vital to one or both parties, strong emotions are to be expected. For some people this raises a significant challenge. You may have been conditioned to hide or suppress strong emotions, but unfortunately, as Carol K. Truman says, "Feelings buried alive never die." As much as you might swallow them deep down inside, put on a brave face and soldier on, when you're under stress in a difficult conversation, strong feelings have a habit of leaking out to infect your words, your tone and your body language.

In the case study, Dina and Toby are being acted on by a potent cocktail of emotions, including frustration, guilt, excitement and hope at the possibility of gaining some freedom from Sheila's continual presence, however well intentioned. Unfortunately, feelings of anxiety, fear and guilt become pre-eminent and prevent them from having the vital conversation.

Now that you understand something of the elements of a vital conversation, the next chapter provides some tools to help you identify the conversations *you* need to have.

3
Your Vital Conversations Audit

S ometimes the conversations you need to have – those that could make the biggest difference to your career, business or personal life – are blatantly obvious; at other times you may be too preoccupied or complacent to recognise these must-have conversations.

To get the maximum benefit from your investment in reading this book, I would strongly recommend that you use this chapter to identify a vital conversation that you need to have in your personal life or professional career. Applying your learning to a real conversation makes all the concepts, strategies and coaching even more relevant to you and your situation. Making connections between what you're reading and your actual life will require more effort, but not only will you retain more of the learning through application, you will also be fully prepared and ready to engage in a vital conversation.

Who do you most need a vital conversation with?

An ideal way to get some momentum is to start your own vital conversations audit. This chapter outlines two processes and some questions that will assist you in clarifying which areas of your work or personal life might benefit from a vital conversation.

Process 1: The Wheel of Life

The Wheel of Life enables you to take a snapshot of your life and break it down into eight key areas. By completing this exercise you get a "helicopter view" and gain further clarity and insight in two ways:

❖ You identify important areas that need your attention.
❖ You realise that to improve those areas you may well require one or more vital conversations.

Start by brainstorming the eight aspects of your life that are most important for you right now.

Two useful categories to help you make your selection are:

❖ The roles you play in life, for example husband/wife, father/mother, brother/sister, son/daughter, manager, leader, colleague, team member, friend, volunteer and so on.
❖ Areas of life that are important to you, for example personal growth, career, home environment, family, friends, money, sense of purpose, fun/pleasure, rest, spirituality and so on.

Choose the aspects that seem most relevant to your life right now and place one on each spoke of the wheel – there's a blank wheel on the next page and a completed example on page 34. The examples given above are not exhaustive, so feel free to choose a role or life area that isn't listed.

Consider each of the eight life dimensions you have chosen in turn. Supposing that 10 (the outer edge of the circle) is "Couldn't be better" and 0 (the circle's centre) is "Couldn't be worse", score yourself on your current level of contentment in each area by marking a dot on each spoke. When you've scored all the areas, join the dots as in the example.

In the example, the person, let's call him Matt, has scored himself 8 on health and fitness, as he has created a disciplined and

The wheel of life

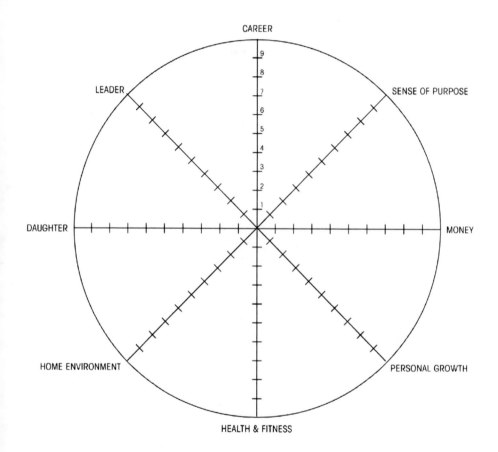

The wheel of life, example

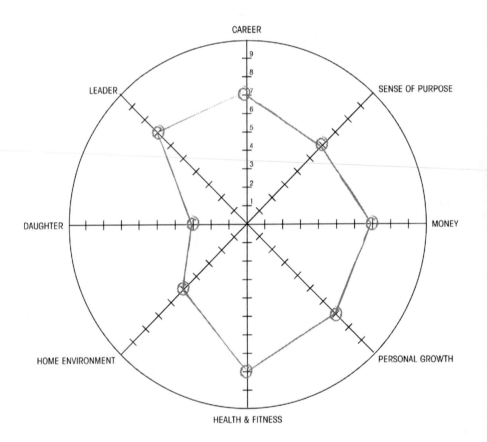

enjoyable exercise routine and feels healthy and fit. However, his role as a father feels like 3 at the moment. He's been so busy in his new job that he hasn't been able to give nearly enough focused time to his teenage daughter. Their communication has been rather fraught and challenging of late around curfew times and her behaviour, which Matt sees as disrespectful.

Having completed the wheel, find time to reflect on it and explore what it conveys to you. Have you become aware of something you didn't expect or recognise? Have certain things that you knew were an issue become even more apparent?

Thought provokers include:

❖ What areas of your wheel concern you?
❖ What conflicts are there between the different life areas or key roles that you play?
❖ Who or what in your life has a negative impact on your scores?
❖ What negative impacts might you have on the lives of others?

Now apply the questions below to your observations from the wheel.

Your vital conversations audit

To continue your own vital conversations audit, ask yourself the following questions, answering only those that feel relevant to you and your wheel of life.

1 Who do I obviously need to have a vital conversation with?
2 What behaviour am I no longer willing to accept from a particular person?
3 Who am I allowing to limit my potential or my personal happiness?
4 What could I gain from such a conversation?

5 In which areas is my silence or procrastination hurting me or other people, my career, my business etc.?

6 Which relationships are hurting the most?

7 What are the benefits for me and the other person from having this conversation?

8 Who isn't meeting my expectations and who is breaking promises to me?

9 Are there situations where roles and responsibilities are unclear or out of date?

10 With whom am I experiencing anger, guilt, worry, fear, frustration, disappointment? Why am I feeling like this?

11 Who do I see as an enemy? Is this in any specific context?

12 Do I have any relationships that feel like lose/win?

13 In which relationships am I being least authentic or do I feel most fake?

14 What am I pretending not to know or acknowledge that would lead to the need for a vital conversation?

15 Who would benefit from my undivided attention or empathy?

16 Who is controlling me?

17 Who am I controlling?

18 Who most deserves an apology or some attention?

19 What issues are not on the table for discussion for my family, project team, board of directors and so on, but should be?

20 Which projects most need a vital conversation to get them back on track?

Take a look at some of your notes and begin to consider who you might want to have a vital conversation with.

Process 2: Relationship mapping

Relationship mapping is a useful visual tool for highlighting potentially challenging relationships and possible vital conversations.

Think of your relationships as like a solar system. You are the equivalent of the sun in the middle with the planets (your key relationships) surrounding you. Some planets are close and warm and others are farther away and colder. In the same way, you have warmer relationships with some people in your life – it's easier to discuss important matters, share feelings, make requests, be yourself and so on – while with others the relationship feels colder, more hostile, discussion feels more difficult, risky or fake.

Think carefully about the key relationships in your life (partner, parent, boss, child, friend, colleague, supplier, key customer and so on) and then map them on page 39 based on how easy or difficult you find it to have a challenging yet vital conversation with them. The degree of difficulty may be context specific, in which case place the relationships on the map based on the particular context or scenario you have in mind. For example, you may be able to chat easily with your mother on everyday stuff, but you may find it impossible to discuss the fact that she does not take her medication consistently, which is affecting her health and increasing your anxiety levels. Place personal relationships on the left and working relationships on the right, and pick at most eight people for each side.

Remember, place the people you struggle to have challenging conversations with farther away from you. Be careful to make a distinction between people you feel you can discuss a sensitive issue with and people you simply get along with: you may be great beer buddies with someone but at the same time not find it easy to have a difficult conversation with them.

Page 38 shows a fictitious example. You can see how this person, let's call her Sarah, struggles to deal with Clive, a project leader. Perhaps they have had unresolved conflicts in the past or she considers Clive very defensive to new ideas. In contrast, Dave (her brother) is positioned close to Sarah – perhaps Dave is a good listener or has always been straightforward and honest.

Relationship map, example

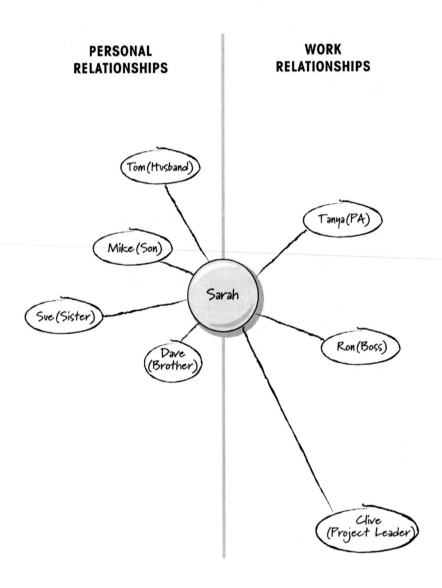

Your relationship map

**PERSONAL
RELATIONSHIPS**

**WORK
RELATIONSHIPS**

me

Once you've put your key relationships on the map, consider some of the following questions in connection with those people who are farthest away from you:

❖ What is the relationship like between you and them right now?
❖ How do you communicate with each other?
❖ How often do you communicate and what modes of communication do you default to (face to face, phone, email, grunts!)?
❖ What judgements or biases do you hold about them?

Now consider whether there's anyone you've placed at a distance who plays a continuous or consistent role in your life and:

❖ Is key to achieving your goals or peace of mind.
❖ Is key for you to have cooperation or collaboration with.
❖ Is making life harder for you than you need it to be.
❖ May also be negatively affected by your style of communication.

Based on your map, who and which conversation needs your attention first?

The vital conversations you need to have

Take some time to go over your notes and answers to all the questions above and decide which conversations are most important for you to have. The rest of this book acts as a guide to prepare you for your next vital conversation.

The template on page 42 is a starting point for getting the bare bones of your vital conversation into focus. As you move through the book I will coach you using a step-by-step process that maps out the conversation in much greater detail.

When you commit your thoughts to paper, you're also making a psychological statement of intent, so completing this template is an important first step in committing yourself to address a particular issue.

Chapter 9 takes you through the first phase of preparing to have that vital conversation, but first we need to look at the foundations that will underpin your approach to such a conversation.

Kick off the vital conversations coaching tool process

Having selected the vital conversation you have chosen to work through, turn to page 231, read the instructions and complete Section 1 of the vital conversations coaching document.

Vital conversations template

Who am I choosing to have a vital conversation with?	
What's the issue? (Be specific.)	
What outcome or solution do I want?	
What are the potential benefits of having this conversation?	
What are the potential pitfalls of having this conversation?	
When will I have this conversation?	
Notes	

Part II

Understanding

4
Shifting to Third-Generation Thinking

"The problems of today will never be solved by the same level of thinking that created them."　　　　　*Albert Einstein*

In more than a decade working with large organisations, I have witnessed leaders and their teams operating at an increasingly frenetic pace. In the pursuit of more productivity, revenue and profit, senior managers, weighed down by their BlackBerry, laptop and other supposedly time-saving devices, can be observed running from one meeting to another in an endless cycle of updating one another. There's lots of communication but not much depth.

With no time for quality conversations, people are becoming more polarised, more impatient, less committed and increasingly frustrated with conflicting interests and competing priorities. Are we actually discussing the real issues? Are we making the time to talk about how we really feel or what's important to us? This diet of high-speed, low-calorie conversations is leading to a lack of joint ownership, diminished trust, flawed solutions and disillusioned teams.

Given today's tough corporate conditions, never has there been a more pressing need for people to challenge the status quo and raise the quality of their communication.

A shift in consciousness

The crucial factor for engaging effectively in vital conversations lies in shifting the way you think. Good interpersonal skills are necessary, but are only part of the equation for creating break-through results in organisations, families or key relationships. In the hands of a surgeon a knife can save lives; in the wrong hands the same knife can hurt or even kill. In the same way, you may have developed an impressive toolbox of interpersonal skills, but if the underlying thinking that drives the use of those skills is command and control or win/lose, in all likelihood the other party will conclude that your intentions are manipulative or at the very least self-serving, leading to suspicion, resentment and inevitably some form of active or passive resistance.

The skills I offer to you in this book could easily be used to influence or coerce someone else into supporting your point of view, but only with short-term success. It is your inner mindset and the values driving your outer behaviour that determine your lasting impact on others. Imagine someone whose predominant mindset is "win don't lose" and someone else whose mindset is "collaboration and mutual understanding". They may both have the same interpersonal skills, but the way they apply them, the results they achieve and their ongoing relationships will be worlds apart.

Key learn: It will be your underlying mindset rather than your skill set that will be the most significant factor in achieving a successful outcome.

Three levels of thinking

Our true mental programming comes to the fore at times of stress. When you squeeze an orange, what comes out is... orange juice.

When you are pressured in a challenging conversation, what mindset leaks out of you? While many people talk a good game around being collaborative and win/win approaches (which reflect what I call third-generation thinking), their behaviour under stress suggests that they're often much more aligned to first- or second-generation thinking.

People operate from three distinct levels of thinking:

❖ First generation – fight or flight.
❖ Second generation – manipulation and control.
❖ Third generation – mutual understanding and compassion.

Let's look at these in more detail.

First-generation thinking: Fight or flight

The behaviour of someone in primitive fight/flight mode can be passive or aggressive. They may unconsciously revert to fight or flight depending on situational factors such as context, perceived or real authority, emotional intensity or historical baggage.

Flight: Overt lose/win, submission

In this mode you either consistently compromise, avoid talking about the real issues or become increasingly passive. Your silence allows others to control the conversation and make unilateral decisions that may have a negative impact on you; in some cases you may even allow the other person to verbally walk over your personal boundaries. When you opt to be compliant and subjugate your own needs, your emotions are usually repressed, leading to deep-seated frustration, anger and sadness. As feelings buried alive never die, you run a serious risk of creating long-term stress, with potentially severe health implications.

Real-life case study: We teach people how to treat us

Vincent left a great IT sales job to start his own software design business when someone he knew outside work was impressed with his business idea and offered to finance the new venture. As the investment was significant, the investor took a 51% stake and Vincent received the remaining 49%.

Both partners were active in the business but it was Vincent who ran it, the investor making occasional appearances at financial reviews. The business grew, producing healthy profits, and within two years had 17 employees.

Then the investor made an unannounced visit to the company when Vincent had taken a day's leave. The following day, he stormed into Vincent's office and laid into him with accusations of weak leadership, poor results and an office where the staff were far too happy to be productive! This feedback was all the more uncalled for as the business was highly productive and very profitable. The partner even insisted that Vincent finish with his girlfriend, as she was seen as a disruptive influence on his commitment to the company.

Unfortunately, Vincent was highly averse to conflict and when under verbal attack became increasingly passive. He did not challenge any of his partner's criticisms.

Over the next three years Vincent was subjected to a weekly lambasting that was tantamount to bullying. Over time his confidence was eroded and, in his words, "I morphed into nothing more than a slave", even agreeing to end his relationship with his longstanding girlfriend. Over those three years he took almost no money out of the business, even in a year in which it made over £500,000 in profits.

Eventually, Vincent had a nervous breakdown and resigned from the business. After several months of further hassle and legal action, he received a settlement of £60,000 for his 49% of a successful company that he had built from the ground up.

When I interviewed Vincent I asked him what he had learnt from such a horrific experience. He replied, "We teach people how to treat us. After several years of being angry at this person, I realised that in that first major tirade from my business partner I did not defend my rightful boundaries." Instead, his passivity had sent the message, "You can get away with abusing me in this way, I will take it."

I will admit that this is an extreme case, but there are many more subtle examples of where we do not challenge the behaviour of others, even when it is having a significantly negative impact on us. Each time we allow that to occur, we are teaching people how to treat us.

Fight: Overt win/lose, coercion

In this mode you are much more adversarial. Typically the fight mindset is driven by an approach centred on rights or power. Rights-based arguments can come from many sources, including defending company rules or procedures, past practices and contractual obligations. When someone is locked into this kind of stance, they focus on promoting their own rights while delegitimising someone else's. For example, it's common for parents in high-stakes conversations with their teenagers to start quoting and enforcing unilateral rules, ranging from the order in which homework and more pleasurable activities are done to curfew times.

A power-based approach is where one or both parties apply whatever resources they can muster on or against the other party. Typical examples are threats, intimidation, physical force, strikes and unilateral decision making. Even guilt trips are based on power. Some adults use physical force to make a child comply; and children (as well as adults) can also be highly adept at using guilt to make things happen their way.

When someone clicks into fight mode their vocal volume increases, they make demands and in the worst cases, as in the case study, they bully and threaten. You can often gauge their emotional intensity in their body language, words and tone of voice, but this is accompanied by little regard for the other person's feelings or psychological safety. People who operate in this mode often get what they want in the short term, yet their relationships are numb, devoid of meaning and transactional in nature.

Thankfully, in the work environment it has become increasingly inappropriate and career limiting to act continually from the first-generation fight stance. However, the virus of fight/flight has mutated into another strain that's harder to spot but has the same mentality at the core of its genetic code.

Second-generation thinking: Manipulate and control

In second-generation thinking the person enters the conversation from a mindset where they have already unilaterally made up their mind about such things as who's right or wrong, what the ideal solution is, who's to blame and so on. Consciously or unconsciously, they have shut down to the possibility that the other person can have information, ideas or a point of view that may have an important influence on the final decision. A second-generation thinker realises that outright confrontation is neither socially nor corporately acceptable. They are also not comfortable with being transparent around their motives or outcomes for the conversation, as this transparency would increase the likelihood of the other person being more resistant or challenging to their unilateral stance. Some of the tell-tale behavioural signs of a second-generation approach include:

❖ Easing into the conversation without actually stating what the issues really are.
❖ Withholding important information that would affect the other person's view of the situation and subsequent decisions.
❖ Not encouraging the other person to challenge their own thinking, ideas or solutions.
❖ The use of fake listening and other covert interpersonal skills that give the impression of caring about the other person's point of view or needs.

Intention is everything

There are literally dozens of books on influencing skills where in my opinion even the authors don't realise that second-generation, manipulate-and-control thinking is at the core of their approach. It's easy to identify this prevailing mindset in the words the authors use: "Show the other person that you're listening by matching their body language", "Pace their tonality and use questions to indicate interest", "Listen so they feel heard". Although all these skills may open the other person up to being influenced, the authors' intention is to convince you to use the techniques to "tee up" the other person so they are more accepting of your unilaterally based solution or decision. For me this lacks transparency, integrity and the possibility of partnership.

It's all about intention. As you will shortly see, if you are attempting to work from a third-generation mindset of genuine mutual understanding and collaboration, you are coming from a very different intent. You don't need to "show" you're listening with the subversive motive of softening the other person up, you simply listen to them because you value them as a human being and are curious to know how your combined thinking could produce a better outcome. Remember, the surgeon and the assassin both have skill with a knife, but they have very different intentions around its application.

The transparency test

Roger Schwarz, one of the world's leading experts on facilitation, shared with me how he coined the term "transparency test" to highlight whether you are consciously or unconsciously using a second-generation mindset, or as he terms it a unilateral control strategy. The test works by asking yourself this question: "Could I be transparent with the other person about the underlying communication strategy I am using in this conversation?"

For example, imagine you are about to enter into dialogue with someone and you want or need that person to accept your solution/point of view. In order to maximise your chances of them buying in to your solution, you decide to use a range of subliminal rapport techniques and a "show them that you're listening" strategy. If you were being totally open/transparent about the intention and methodology behind your communication strategy, the initial conversation with the other person might go like this:

"Hi Jim. It's really important for me to get you on board with my way of thinking. To do this I'm going to match your body language and imitate the pace and pitch of your voice, as this is psychologically proven to make you feel like we have great rapport with each other and that you can trust me. I'm then going to ask you some questions and paraphrase back some of your key concerns, as this should make you feel that I care about what's important to you. By doing this I'm hoping you will be more relaxed and open to my solution, which of course, in my mind, is the superior one."

If you think this sounds farcical, I would agree with you! As you can see, you couldn't share this approach without the other person becoming wary, as they realise that you have dubious intentions. However, this is often the conscious or unconscious strategy behind many attempts at dialogue where high stakes and differing opinions are likely. A covert approach may work on those who are submissive or don't consider the issues important, but in a vital conversation such a strategy can create the very defensiveness and resistance that the second-generation approach is trying to avoid.

Case study

Mary, who manages Carlos, wants to provide some feedback on a recent presentation he gave to a prospective new client. Based on second-generation thinking, Mary has already made a unilateral decision about what Carlos failed to do and where he needs to improve. Her strategy is to probe with questions that "allow" Carlos (for his own future benefit, of course) to realise the improvements Mary knows he should make.

The conversation goes as follows...

MARY: I've been meaning to talk to you about the recent client meeting at Norcom last week. How do you think your part of the presentation went?
CARLOS: Oh pretty well, I think the client appreciated my innovative ideas.

At this point Mary is having another conversation, only this one is taking place in her head. This is what I would call a private inner conversation, or PIC for short:

MARY PIC: *Come on, Carlos, even someone as thick skinned as you could see that the manufacturing director wasn't convinced about the viability of the solution you put forward. Looks like I will have to make this feedback more focused.*

MARY: What about the manufacturing director? Do you think he may have been unsure about your answers to his questions?

By now Carlos is starting to have his own inner conversation.

CARLOS PIC: *Hmm, where's Mary going with this?*

CARLOS: Mary, you know how conservative manufacturing directors are, they're paid to be pessimistic about the operational effectiveness of a leading-edge solution.

MARY PIC: *Typical Carlos, laying the problem at the feet of the client and not admitting his own lack of preparation.*

MARY: Actually Carlos, this is no joking matter. I think your lack of preparation might well have cost us the business. I want to see you prepare more thoroughly in future.

CARLOS PIC: *OK, so this is where she's going. What she needs to understand is that without my ideas and passion, this company wouldn't have any clients.*

CARLOS: My prep and approach are spot on. Try to find someone else whose creativity has won us seven accounts this year!

MARY PIC: *I knew he would get defensive. I wanted to do this the nice way, but I'm just going to have to spell it out.*

The case study highlights how second-generation thinking creates the very defensiveness Mary wanted to avoid. She is still unconscious of the fact that it was her second-generation thinking that evoked his resistance in the first place.

Notice how quickly the veneer of this kind of approach can be rubbed away. As Mary's frustration increases, she regresses to a first-generation, power-based approach, telling Carlos unilaterally that he has to change. To be fair to Mary, she may have recently attended a managers' coaching workshop where she was trained to ask questions before giving her point of view. When you're engaged in giving a difficult message or feedback, my recommendation is initially to hold back from using coaching tools and instead be transparent from the start about your intentions for the conversation.

Mini exercise: Reflecting on your default mindset
This exercise is useful for identifying or acknowledging second-generation thinking.

Cast your mind back to a couple of high-stakes conversations you had before reading this book. Try to remember your mindset as you entered the conversation and how that affected your behaviour as it progressed. On reflection, ask yourself if you would have been able to share your underlying communication strategy with the other person. Was your truest intention win/win? Did you listen with a genuine desire to find information that would alter your original take on the issues and solutions?

If you found that it would have been impossible or embarrassing to be transparent with the underlying communication strategy you chose, or decide on reflection that it was manipulative, then you were most likely coming from a second-generation mindset.

Third-generation thinking: The 7 Cs

"Out beyond ideas of right and wrong there is a field, I will meet you there."   *Rumi*

Evolving from second- to third-generation thinking is challenging. It requires you to let go of two patterns of thought that drive behaviour in vital but difficult conversations:

❖ Being right, or its close cousin, not being wrong.
❖ The need to win.

In the British educational system, young people are conditioned from a tender age, being praised for getting things right and ignored, shamed or punished for getting things wrong. Although some schools are slowly moving away from this carrot-and-stick approach, our children are under continual pressure to get the right answers, whether in the exam hall or the classroom.

The need to be right is often reinforced at business school. When MBA graduates were interviewed, many said that their lecturers encouraged students to shoot down each other's business ideas or points of view. Take a look at the curriculum of many MBA programmes and see if you can find any significant investment of time in the subject of conflict resolution or "interests-based" facilitation. Yet these missing elements are core leadership skills for developing team unity, fostering creativity, increasing employee engagement and relationship building.

Human beings are highly motivated to move away from painful experiences. Being wrong or being told that you are wrong leads to uncomfortable emotions and self-doubt. Ask yourself: "When I'm discussing something I believe strongly about, how does it feel to be explicitly or implicitly told my ideas, viewpoints or feelings are wrong?" Is it any wonder our habitual response is to feel disrespected, angry, frustrated, humiliated or even afraid?

If you choose to stay in this right/wrong mode of thinking, you have two options. You either avoid the pain of being wrong by fighting your corner and proving how right you actually are (therefore making the other person wrong, and guess how they will feel about that?), or you take the flight option and decide not to openly contest opinions, reducing the possibility of being publicly wrong yet having to bear the inner stress, frustration and resentment that percolate within you because you haven't been heard. Do you have to remain stuck in a second-generation paradigm that keeps you oscillating between the two stress-inducing opposing poles of wrong and right?

Buddha gave an accurate if somewhat oversimplified answer to this dilemma. He said "Don't cling" and "If you cling you suffer." If you relate this to your vital conversation, you may have to let go of needing to be right or clinging to your solution or point of view. This doesn't mean that you don't bring your ideas, needs, concerns and fears to the table, but it does call for you to be open to new information, alternative solutions and the possibility that you may be missing information or operating on incorrect assumptions.

You certainly don't need to walk away from what's important to you, but your mindset has to change from consolidating and defending your position to sharing, enquiring, adjusting and broadening your view.

You may be thinking that second generation has served you well so far and that you've been very successful at getting what you want from other people. But you can still suffer even when you win. Can you recall a time when you won your argument, made someone else wrong or used your position or authority to force someone to comply or say sorry? Did it honestly feel good in the long run? Did the other person respect you, trust you or love you? Did it enrich your future interactions with that person? Mutual understanding, respect, collaboration and a search for joint solutions are more concrete foundations for a successful long-term relationship, and they are the hallmarks of third-generation thinking.

A blueprint for third-generation thinking

When you encounter someone who has made the transition to third-generation thinking, you don't just know it, you *feel* it. They have the courage to talk openly about issues and yet they demonstrate little or no ego, even when you challenge their thinking or openly disagree with their viewpoint. They place the relationship at the heart of their attempts to communicate, holding a deep-seated intention to achieve a mutually beneficial outcome through the relationship rather than at the expense of it. They work hard to understand your view of the world and encourage both sides to explore different ways of finding solutions. Third-generation thinking is not reserved for intellectuals, spiritual types or business leaders, but can be developed by anyone who realises that the conversation is at the heart of the relationship.

7 Cs	Underlying assumptions	Strategies/skills/behaviours
Control (self)	My self-awareness and emotional state management have a major impact on the success of my vital conversations	Develop emotional state management and self-awareness skills
Clarity	I am clear why I am having this conversation	Qualify thinking and motives before engaging in a vital conversation
	Both parties need all relevant information to make an informed decision	Communicate all necessary information. Use clear examples and get a shared understanding of what important words and concepts mean
Compassion	The other person is communicating at their best; if they knew better they would do better	Respectfully enquire into other people's motives and reasoning, rather than only judging external behaviour or decisions
	It is OK for me and the other party to have strong feelings	Develop the capability to label and talk about strong emotions, both mine and theirs
	I accept that I will make mistakes in vital conversations and that's part of my learning journey	Use a learning journal to turn mistakes and challenging moments into opportunities for growth
Curiosity	I bring some information to this conversation, others may have different information	Test my and others' assumptions
	Each person is likely to see things that the other does not or may have missed	Make my thinking transparent, including sharing my reasoning and motives
	Differences are opportunities for understanding and learning	Enquire into others' different views, feelings and needs

7 Cs	Underlying assumptions	Strategies/skills/ behaviours
Courage	I have the right to communicate my ideas, needs, feelings and point of view My own thinking may be incorrect and should be challenged I have the right to enquire into and compassionately challenge another's point of view	Share feelings and make clear requests about my needs and goals where appropriate Interrogate my own view of reality and encourage others to challenge my thinking Develop enquiry and listening skills
Collaboration	I strive to meet both parties' interests/needs wherever possible	Focus on people's interests first and create options and solutions second
Commitment	Both parties are accountable for their commitments and promises	Seek clarity and accountability on agreements, next steps, actions and timelines

Above is an overview of third-generation thinking. It starts with the creation of seven values, an internal compass to guide you through vital conversations. There will be times in the heat of challenging dialogue where you lose your way or the other person takes the conversation to a place that is uncomfortable for you. The seven guiding values, or 7 Cs for short, are the deep mental programming that drives resourceful behaviour. When you're lost at night in difficult conversational woods, these values and the approach connected to them will light your path and see you through.

The table is in three columns. Each guiding value is underpinned by one or more mental assumptions, described in the middle column. The strategies, skills and behaviours in the third column are the physical manifestation of thinking that flows from the third-generation approach. It is this combination that creates a climate of mutual understanding and collaboration. As we journey together through the chapters in this book I will look in greater depth at how these values, assumptions and behaviours align to improve your confidence and capability in a vital conversation.

If you're ready and committed to make the journey to a third-generation perspective, amazing things can start to happen. You often elicit a surprisingly different response from other people, altering previously unproductive patterns of behaviour or breaking through conversational roadblocks to mutually beneficial solutions. However, you must be the first to change your thinking and approach; as Gandhi said, "We must become the change we want to see in the world." You cannot wait for the other person to change, you have to make the shift.

Delivering a fait accompli

When I cover third-generation thinking in my workshops, at least one delegate will raise concerns over how it fits with the scenario where you are communicating a decision that is unilateral and the other party cannot change the outcome. How can you be collaborative in a situation of that kind?

Let's take the example of letting someone know that they are being made redundant. If the decision is essential to protect the long-term survival of the business and the wider workforce's employment, I would agree that you cannot have a collaborative discussion with that person about whether they lose their job. You can, however, still bring third-generation thinking into the conversation. For instance, having shared the bad news, you can still co-design how you have the conversation (collaboration). You can still have compassion for the other person's feelings and the curiosity to understand where they are at having heard the bad news. (There's more about bad-news conversations in Chapter 14.)

Nevertheless, nine times out of ten you will be engaged in vital conversations where the greatest impediment to you using a third-generation approach will be your own habitual conditioning, not the context or circumstances you find yourself in.

Case study

Let's go back to Mary and Carlos. This is how the start of the conversation might have gone if Mary had approached the conversation from a third-generation mindset.

MARY: Hi Carlos, I've been meaning to talk to you about the recent client meeting at Norcom last week. Is this a good time to talk?

CARLOS: Sure, what's on your mind?

MARY: At the meeting I was uneasy with the way you fielded the manufacturing director's questions and I think it had an impact on our chances of winning that piece of business. I'd like to share with you my concerns, and then I want to hear from you to find out if you see my feedback differently. How does that sound to you?

CARLOS: Oh come on, Mary, you know how pedantic those manufacturing guys can get around new implementations. My creativity is bound to make some people nervous.

MARY: Your creativity is a major asset to this firm and the manufacturing director did ask a lot of questions, and even so I would still like to share my concerns with you.

CARLOS: Well, if I'm being honest he did ask some pretty tough questions. What was your take on how that part of the meeting went?

I'm not saying that the feedback Mary gives will be well received, since even perfectly delivered feedback can be hard to hear. What the discussion does show, however, is that Mary was able to be transparent and up front with what she wants to discuss. It wasn't brutal and yet she still had the courage to stay with her aim of sharing her concerns. She had compassion for how Carlos may have been feeling and, crucially, she demonstrated collaboration and curiosity in the way she offered him the chance to give his version of how he perceived the meeting and her feedback. We did not hear the end of that vital conversation, but we might have seen Mary demonstrating clarity and commitment, making sure that both of them were clear on what changes or next steps were agreed.

Finally, Mary demonstrated self-control. She had the self-awareness to remain calm and confident. Without effective emotional state management it is almost impossible to engage in a vital conversation effectively, let alone approach it from a third-generation mindset.

Sceptical?

It's OK if you are – for many years I was too. In my previous career in IT sales and management, a motivational speaker would be wheeled out each year at the annual kick-off meeting in which the latest team buzzwords were trotted out. One of the all-time favourites that made several guest appearances over the years was "Think win/win!"

Although there was a genuinely positive intent to act in collaborative, win/win ways with one's team members and customers, the reality of achieving collaboration was much more challenging for two reasons. First, we had no knowledge of how to make that significant shift in mindset to collaborative third-generation thinking, therefore the skills that were passed on were inevitably employed from a first- or second-generation, win/lose mindset.

Secondly, even if a real effort was made to create the necessary paradigm shift, the tools or skills we possessed weren't nearly comprehensive or practised enough to handle challenging situations where the other party was operating from a determined win/lose stance. Inevitably in these situations we often ended up either accommodating the other person's wishes, or at best ending up in some kind of middle-ground compromise that was rarely satisfactory or committed to by either party.

As you can imagine, it didn't take too many of these experiences for our belief in collaborative dialogue to be compromised, leaving us with the view that collaboration was a worthy ideal, but not actually possible in the real world.

I can't promise that every vital conversation you have will turn out to be effortlessly collaborative; the reality is the other person is unlikely to come from that thinking and you will have to be very self-aware to remain in that mode yourself. However, if you are willing to give the third-generation mindset a fair crack, then the skills and process offered in these pages are sufficiently practical and robust for you to find that win/win is achievable far more often than you may imagine.

5
Gaining Self-Mastery

"We need to move from unconscious stress reactions to conscious stress responses."   *Jon Kabit-zin*

Before you can influence the success of your vital conversations, you must first learn how to influence yourself. Mastering emotions such as anger, fear and frustration and tapping into inner resources such as confidence, courage and compassion are skills you can learn. In Chapters 5–8 you will learn how to raise your self-awareness and in turn reduce unhelpful negative patterns of thinking that affect your ability to engage in productive dialogue. You will take on board strategies that will build your confidence and courage and enable you to access your full potential and maximise the changes of a successful outcome.

You may be tempted to skip these chapters because of an understandable urge to get stuck into planning your conversation. But don't! Not investing time in the development of your emotional self-mastery results in the following very real consequences:

❖ Too much self-generated fear leads to procrastination over having the conversation.
❖ Your nerves get the better of you and you shy away from talking about the real issues.
❖ High levels of anxiety begin to shut down your brain, leaving you unable to find the right words or skills to maintain effective dialogue.
❖ High levels of anger can generate domineering behaviour and words that hurt rather than heal.

❖ Unacknowledged emotions such as frustration affect the clarity of your thinking and you think the worst of others and their motives.

❖ In an unresourceful state you become more inflexible and less collaborative.

In addition, if you can't establish and maintain a resourceful state of mind you may struggle to:

❖ Develop the compassion that allows you to listen without judging and genuinely see the other person's pain or point of view.

❖ Have the courage to stay true to what is important to you and respectfully challenge the other person's behaviour, thinking or decisions.

❖ Remain calm and curious when the other person is highly emotional, inflexible, dominant and so on.

I cannot emphasise enough the importance of this section of the book and its potential impact on your capability to engage in successful vital conversations. I urge you to practise the strategies for self-mastery so that your ability to influence yourself will become the bedrock on which you build the rest of your conversation.

Case study: The mind–body connection

Its 9.55 a.m. and John has five minutes before a meeting with Sarah, where he will attempt to talk about how her aggressive behaviour in meetings is alienating her from the team. By 9.58 John's palms are beginning to sweat, he has huge tension in his jaw and shoulders, his heartbeat has quickened significantly and his breathing is quick yet shallow.

Sarah arrives and after the usual pleasantries John attempts to begin the vital conversation. Rather than communicating in the way he had rehearsed, however, he finds it really difficult to be clear and concise; instead, he starts to talk in a much more indirect way about the issue. "I don't have a problem with your style, but others in the team find you too positive or well... forward, er, you know what I mean?"

At an unconscious level Sarah picks up on John's anxiety and swiftly begins to generate her own unresourceful emotions. Questions begin to surface in her mind: "So who exactly has the problem with me? What's wrong with being forward and positive?"

Quickly John is placed on the back foot, with Sarah demanding to know who has an issue with her. John is overwhelmed as the conversation goes from bad to worse. At this point he is facing what might be termed an emotional hijack. He has got to a point where he simply can't think straight; he ends up in a first-generation response and becomes increasingly passive. Unfortunately, under stress Sarah has her own habitual patterns of behaviour and also becomes emotionally hijacked. Her defensive response is anger rather than fear and she is in fight mode, firing angry questions and statements at John that he has no cognitive capacity or capability to handle.

When you begin to understand the mind—body connection (see oposite) it is easier to see why so many vital conversations derail. Ultimately, John can't control how Sarah reacts in this conversation, but if he knows how to influence his own emotional state regardless of that reaction, he has a real chance of creating a more productive dialogue and outcome.

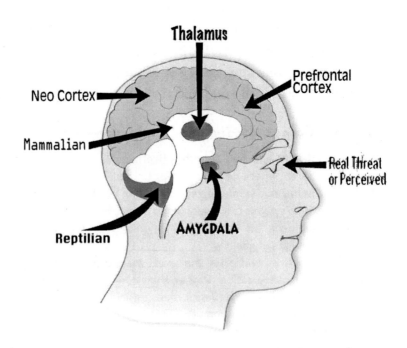

The science behind our emotions

So how do we end up in an emotional straitjacket? The answer can be found by looking at a part of the brain that is only the size of an almond. In essence, your brain has four interlinked parts. First to evolve was the reptilian brain; then came the mammalian (or limbic) brain, which as one of its many functions is the emotional centre; finally, over tens of thousands of years, the cortex and prefrontal cortex brain emerged, which gave the human race a unique advantage over all other life forms, the capacity for conscious reasoning and hence the ability to observe and instantaneously adapt their own behaviour.

Within the mammalian brain sits this almond-sized object known as the amygdala. It serves a critical role as a protective guardian, issuing orders to the rest of the body at incredible speed in life or death situations. If, for instance, you accidentally stepped out in front of a bus, it would be your amygdala that (hopefully) ordered your entire body to leap backwards in the blink of an eye.

This process depends on the way the brain routes information. (You may find the simplified brain diagram opposite helpful.) In the above scenario, you take in visual data about the speeding bus. The information journey begins with activation of one of the senses, in this case vision, which is routed to the thalamus. The thalamus monitors and sorts all sensory information (except smell). Like an air traffic controller, its job is to keep the signals moving.

In a non-life-threatening situation, say the bus is still 200 metres away, the thalamus directs the impulse to the high reasoning part of our brain, the neocortex, or specifically in this case the visual cortex, for processing. The cortex "thinks" about the impulse and makes sense of it: "Aha, a speeding large object! I should get reasonably excited about this." That signal is then sent to the amygdala, which refines the fight/flight response and regulates your emotions. The hypothalamus, which adjoins the thalamus, is also an important member of this emotional orchestra. It tells the brain what is happening inside the body, including activating the pituitary gland. This directs your adrenal glands to release the stress hormones of adrenalin and cortisol if you are faced with immediate danger or fail to respond in a rational way to a perceived stressful situation. It's important to realise that when you're under stress your emotional state is not just on a neural trip, your entire body is having a simultaneous biochemical trip as well.

In a physically threatening situation, the thalamus has a different reaction. Like any skilled air traffic controller, the thalamus can react quickly to a potential threat. In high-risk scenarios, it bypasses the cortex (the thinking brain) and the signal goes straight to the amygdala. The amygdala then sends chemical messengers via the hypothalamus and the body gets ready for fight or flight, rerouting blood and energy away from the brain and vital organs to the muscular and skeletal system, which then does its job of removing or handling the imminent threat.

The challenge is that the amygdala cannot tell the difference between a physical, emotional or perceived threat. In vital conversations where the stakes and emotions are running high, it's very easy for one or both parties to feel threatened or scared. Unfortunately, what you see, hear and perceive in these circumstances stimulates the thalamus and the amygdala kicks in before your prefrontal cortex has the chance to think the situation through rationally. In a blink of an eye, a hundred thousand years of ancestry goes to your defence and the flight/fight physical response kicks in. The higher functions of the neocortex reasoning brain temporarily shut down and you either become passive (flight), as happened to John, or you flip to being aggressive, as was Sarah's inevitable fate. It's particularly damaging to the relationship when one or both parties are hijacked into fight mode, as with little conscious reasoning they begin to "brain fart", a term I use to describe people who just blurt out judgements, harsh words, criticism or foul language, all of which hurt the relationship and kill the potential for a successful conversation.

Once you have been emotionally hijacked, you can become emotionally and physically stuck in a reinforcing loop, keeping you in an unresourceful mode of being. Your body often becomes very tense. Under a physical attack (the amygdala's original purpose) you would be running or fighting and continually dissipating the stress hormones of adrenalin and cortisol. A difficult conversation is a physically more passive situation and the stress hormones are not easily released from the body, therefore they build up. This creates what is called a "cybernetic closed loop". The build-up of stress hormones creates further tension in various parts of the body, sending signals back to the brain that all is not well and generating more emotion (fear, frustration, anger and so on). Emotion focuses attention, so if you're having strong negative emotions it tends to direct your focus or mental attention to what's negative or in your view wrong, unfair or scary. This continues to fire off the hypothalamus, which sends out further messages to your pituitary glands to excrete more cortisol and adrenalin, which exaggerates your tension and stress and so the reinforcing loop goes on.

Being in this state for more than a few minutes is exhausting. In physically threatening situations the fight/flight scenario usually lasts for only a few seconds, but without effective emotional state management it may go on for the whole duration of a vital conversation.

The architect of your own downfall

So now you know the biological background to being emotionally hijacked – but in a vital conversation, how do you end up getting into that mess in the first place? In a moment I will revisit John and Sarah, but first it will help you to understand how your mind works for or against you in these high-octane conversations.

Three major factors that drive your emotional reaction to real or perceived threats are:

❖ Your internal dialogue (the way you talk to yourself).
❖ The mental movies or visualisations you create in your mind.
❖ Your body's reaction to thinking.

The best way I know of highlighting the effect this trio has is by sharing a scenario that most of us will have experienced at some point in our life. You're alone in your home. It's 3 a.m. and you're fast asleep when a loud noise wakes you. After the initial shock of being startled, your inner voice begins to talk to you: "What was that? Hmmm, probably something fell over, maybe it was the cat coming through the flap, everything's fine, go back to sleep." If that's what you say to yourself you probably fall swiftly back into a slumber.

But what if your inner voice says something more sinister: "What was that? Oh my God, someone's broken in, what do they want, what will they do to me?" That kicks off a process. The inner dialogue stimulates your imagination and you begin to visualise who the burglar might be. If your inner dialogue says "It sounds like a mad axeman who's come to brutally murder me", then that's the mental movie you create. You begin to see the axeman bursting through your door – I'll leave the rest of this self-generated horror flick to your own imagination.

Under stress, your mind can't tell the difference between something vividly imagined and something real. So your mental assumption about the mad axeman creates enough of a perceived threat to fire off your amygdala and the body enters the cycle of becoming increasingly tense, with shallow breathing, increased heart rate and so on. Once you're emotionally hostage to your thinking, you either hide under the covers (flight) or, fuelled with adrenalin, pick up the nearest available sharp object and go on the hunt for the intruder!

Case study: A self-fulfilling prophecy

Let's return to John. It's 9.55 a.m. In the last five minutes before Sarah walks in, John may well be unaware that his mental elaborations are seriously undermining his chances of a productive conversation. It's easy to see how his inner dialogue may have been saying: "I really hope I don't screw this up", "What happens if Sarah doesn't take this well and I end up getting the sharp side of her tongue?" or "Knowing Sarah, she's bound to lose it". This creates movies in John's mind of an angry, possibly even vindictive Sarah. Before long, that starts to create fear and anxiety, leading to tension, shallow breathing and a fast heartbeat. John is beginning to be emotionally hijacked and he hasn't even started the conversation!

Although he's stressed, John probably has very little conscious awareness that his brain and body are beginning to enter a downward spiral. So at 10 a.m., feeling very anxious, he screws up the start of the conversation, gets an adverse reaction from Sarah and the whole dialogue starts to play out in a very similar fashion to the nightmare he visualised five minutes earlier. John can even reflect later on the conversation and say "I knew the conversation would turn out like that", yet unwittingly he played a significant role in creating that destiny.

Mini exercise: Destructive thinking patterns
Listed opposite (with thanks to Michael Chakalson, a leading light in mindfulness-based stress reduction, for permission to reproduce them) are some of the most common stress-inducing thinking patterns, with an example of the type of inner dialogue that results from each. The inner dialogue creates a mental movie and generates unresourceful feelings.

Take a look at each one and ask yourself: "Have I ever been guilty of thinking this way?"

❖ Mind reading (untested assumptions): "He thinks my ideas are stupid."

❖ Crystal ball gazing (projecting into the future): "This is going to be a total nightmare."

❖ Overdramatising the negative: "My manager is destroying my credibility."

❖ Overgeneralising: "She's always putting me down."

❖ Being judgemental: "I'm such a doormat" or "They are so inconsiderate."

❖ Blaming: "They created this problem."

Over the next 48 hours, attempt to catch your inner dialogue using these or similar thinking patterns. Begin to notice if you find yourself blaming, generalising, mind reading etc. Simply becoming aware of it is often enough to stop that type of destructive thinking from taking hold.

It's important to realise that you can get emotionally hijacked at any point in the vital conversations process. You may be preparing for the conversation and very strong feelings begin to surface due to something the other person may have done or said in the past. Alternatively, you may be 20 minutes into the conversation and the other party passes judgement, calling you unprofessional, political or selfish. Sometimes all it takes is a word, a look or a harsh tone and you're immediately in an emotionally unresourceful place.

How you respond when that happens will make all the difference in achieving a successful outcome to your vital conversations. I will talk more extensively about how you avoid becoming emotionally hijacked in the following three chapters, and the first step in building your capacity to respond resourcefully is the art of becoming increasingly self-aware.

6
Developing Self-Awareness

"He who knows others is wise. He who knows himself is enlightened."

Lao Tzu

Morihei Ueshiba was the founder of aikido, a martial art that takes the energy and aggression of an attacker and uses that very same energy to disable the opponent. Master Ueshiba was famous for his incredible balance, yet when students asked him how he had achieved such a level of mastery, he would reply humbly, "I am not a master of balance but I am quite good at regaining my balance." He understood that losing one's balance in martial arts or in wider aspects of life is the norm and cannot be avoided. The ability to regain your composure swiftly is what's important.

It would be naive to think that a high-stakes interaction like a vital conversation will be plain sailing. There will be occassions when you feel off balance when the other party does or says something that unsettles your composure. The question is how you regain your emotional and cognitive balance, and to do this you must first become more self-aware.

Under the surface

To understand the deeper psychology that drives your behaviour, a powerful visual metaphor is an iceberg. As you may be aware, only about 10–15% of an iceberg is usually visible above the waterline, with the vast majority hidden below the ocean's surface.

Look at the diagram above and you'll see that I've put "Behaviour" and "Results" above the waterline. This is because when two people are in a conversation, that's the only part of the interaction that is directly visible. If I was observing a video recording of your vital conversation I could hear the questions you asked and the tone you used. I could observe your body language. I could even evaluate the results you were getting based on the quality of the dialogue and rapport. However, without directly asking you I could only guess or make assumptions about how you were feeling and what you were thinking but not necessarily saying.

In the heat of a difficult conversation, you are often so caught up in its content, either justifying your point of view or becoming frustrated with the other person's stance on a certain issue, that you pay little attention to powerful influencing factors deep within you, below the waterline. Yet it is at these deeper levels that you have the opportunity to exercise your unique human gift for self-observation, which is so critical to how you manage and use your emotions.

There are three psychological levels below the waterline of the iceberg and I start with the one closest to the surface, feelings.

Broadening your emotional bandwidth

"As none can see the wind but in its effects on the trees, neither can we see the emotions but in their effects on the face and body."

Nathaniel LeTonnerre

Marshall Rosenberg, the founder of the Center for Nonviolent Communication, says, "Our repertoire for calling people names is often larger than our vocabulary of words that allow us to clearly describe our emotional state."

In my opinion, society still undervalues emotional intelligence. EQ, as it is often termed, is a massive subject in itself, but in essence it's a measure of someone's capability to manage their own emotions while being aware and empathic to the emotional states of others. Unless you attended a Montessori, Rudolph Steiner or similar school, it's highly unlikely that you were given any formal training in this kind of intelligence. It's also possible that you had parents or guardians who did not encourage the open expression of emotions. In your working and professional life, the organisation's culture may be uncomfortable with feelings, seeing people who reveal their emotions as needy or weak. So a mixture of parenting, societal and corporate conditioning often represses the open expression of feelings. Yet in your bid to engage successfully in vital conversations, you need at the very least to acknowledge powerful feelings, and in certain circumstances actually share those feelings with the other person.

In my workshops I ask delegates to identify emotions they were not encouraged to express in their childhood. A common example is not being allowed to show disappointment or to be seen as ungrateful. Depending on the degree to which their parents suppressed that emotion in them (usually through the mechanisms of guilt, shaming or verbal or physical aggression), delegates begin to gain insight into why in certain contexts they find it difficult to engage in conversations where they need to express disappointment.

When I'm involved in mediation, whether it's warring neighbours in a deprived area or senior managers in a multibillion-pound organisation, the parties involved can become frustrated as they struggle to find words to describe accurately how they feel. They may end up making quite general statements. When someone says "I feel bad about such-and-such", it's difficult to pinpoint on the emotional spectrum what *bad* really means. Is it actually sad, depressed or angry? If you have a limited range of emotional labels, you can find it difficult to express how you're feeling and it's even more challenging to convey those emotions in a way that the other person can hear without becoming defensive. In fact, it's more common to express feelings incorrectly, in the form of either a diagnosis of how you think the other person is behaving or a moralistic judgement. For example, someone who is feeling sad or frustrated because the other person is not open to hearing their point of view may say, "I feel that you just don't care what's important to me" or "I feel that you're too selfish to listen to what I have to say." As you can imagine, this misdescription of feelings rarely goes down well with the other person. When was the last time you responded well to being called selfish?

Mini exercise: Know your emotional footprint
To increase your ability to engage in vital conversations, it's essential to build your vocabulary of feelings. It's also useful to become aware of and acknowledge any emotions that you either suppress, deny or would be uncomfortable talking about. If you remain unconscious to these blind spots, you run the risk of behaving in unresourceful or inauthentic ways when such emotions are triggered by what the other person says or by their previous actions and behaviour.

So to help you further along that path, overleaf is a list of commonly experienced feelings. This list is not exhaustive, but it will be useful when you complete the section on feelings in the vital conversation coaching toolkit.

AFFECTIONATE
compassionate
friendly
loving
open-hearted
sympathetic
tender
warm

CONFIDENT
empowered
open
proud
safe
secure

ENGAGED
absorbed
alert
curious
engrossed
enchanted
entranced
fascinated
interested
intrigued
involved
spellbound
stimulated

INSPIRED
amazed
awed
wonder

EXCITED
amazed
animated
ardent
aroused
astonished
dazzled
eager
energetic
enthusiastic
giddy
invigorated
lively

passionate
surprised
vibrant

EXHILARATED
blissful
ecstatic
elated
enthralled
exuberant
radiant
rapturous
thrilled

GRATEFUL
appreciative
moved
thankful
touched

HOPEFUL
expectant
encouraged
optimistic

JOYFUL
amused
delighted
glad
happy
jubilant
pleased
tickled

PEACEFUL
calm
clear-headed
comfortable
centred
content
equanimous
fulfilled
mellow
quiet
relaxed
relieved
satisfied
serene

still
tranquil
trusting

REFRESHED
enlivened
rejuvenated
renewed
rested
restored
revived

AFRAID
apprehensive
dread
foreboding
frightened
mistrustful
panicked
petrified
scared
suspicious
terrified
wary
worried

ANNOYED
aggravated
dismayed
disgruntled
displeased
exasperated
frustrated
impatient
irritated
irked

ANGRY
enraged
furious
incensed
indignant
irate
livid
outraged
resentful

cont.

AVERSION
animosity
appalled
contempt
disgusted
dislike
hate
horrified
hostile
repulsed

CONFUSED
ambivalent
baffled
bewildered
dazed
hesitant
lost
mystified
perplexed
puzzled
torn

DISCONNECTED
alienated
aloof
apathetic
bored
cold
detached
distant
distracted
indifferent
numb
removed
uninterested
withdrawn

DISQUIET
agitated
alarmed
discombobulated
disconcerted
disturbed
perturbed
rattled
restless

shocked
startled
surprised
troubled
turbulent
turmoil
uncomfortable
uneasy
unnerved
unsettled
upset

EMBARRASSED
ashamed
chagrined
flustered
guilty
mortified
self-conscious

FATIGUE
beat
burnt out
depleted
exhausted
lethargic
listless
sleepy
tired
weary
worn out

PAIN
agony
anguished
bereaved
devastated
grief
heartbroken
hurt
lonely
miserable
regretful
remorseful

SAD
depressed

dejected
despair
despondent
disappointed
discouraged
disheartened
forlorn
gloomy
heavy hearted
hopeless
melancholy
unhappy
wretched

TENSE
anxious
cranky
distressed
distraught
edgy
fidgety
frazzled
irritable
jittery
nervous
overwhelmed
restless
stressed out

VULNERABLE
fragile
guarded
helpless
insecure
leery
reserved
sensitive
shaky

YEARNING
envious
jealous
longing
nostalgic
pining
wistful

Take some time now to raise your awareness of your emotional footprint by looking at the list and reflecting on the following questions:

❖ Are there any that you are uncomfortable experiencing or would find it hard to admit to having?
❖ Can you identify any feelings that you were either discouraged from expressing, or shamed or ignored if you did, in your childhood, school or career?
❖ Are there any distraction strategies you employ to avoid feeling certain emotions?
❖ Which would you find hardest to express in a vital conversation?

Taking responsibility for your own feelings

As discussed, most people receive very little training on accurately observing and acknowledging feelings. A further common mistake is to attribute your strong feelings solely to the other person's behaviour or actions, by confusing stimulus with response.

A great example of this confusion in everyday life is the common occurrence in Britain of a commuter train arriving late, and being so full of passengers there are no seats for those about to board. The train being late and jam-packed is the stimulus; how people respond is an individual experience. Some are angry: "This is outrageous! I pay a lot of money for my season ticket and I can't even get a seat!" Others are anxious: "I will be late for that crucial meeting." A rare few may even look at the human sardine tin and feel compassion for those who are not enjoying the journey. Another person who is a day away from retirement may be ecstatic or depressed that this is their last commute.

So the same stimulus can create a myriad of responses and yet we often believe that a particular external stimulus is forcing us into a specific feeling. Although it's challenging at times, ultimately you choose your emotional response. However, without continual vigiliance it's easy to absolve yourself and transfer this responsibility to others.

Instead of saying "She makes me so angry turning up late for meetings", it's more responsible and resourceful to own your emotion and describe how the behaviour affects you: "I become angry when Sheila enters the room after the meeting has started as we have to cover old ground again and we lose precious time."

Blaming is disempowering

If you blame others for your emotional state, then by default you mentally relinquish control over your ability to respond in more resourceful ways. When you say "She makes me angry", you are destined to be emotionally enslaved, at the mercy of other people's decisions or behaviour. For a significant percentage of society this way of thinking has become the norm. As eminent psychologist Martin Seligman has proved in his research, people become "learned helpless" and no longer realise or believe that they are capable of responding differently to a situation or person. This perceived lack of choice also creates another disabling side effect. If you feel that you have no choice, you are much more likely to have an immature mental response. There is also an increased chance of regressing into first-generation, fight or flight thinking, where you either become passive or go on the attack.

Taking full responsibility for the entire spectrum of your emotions is empowering. By taking this stance, over time you become more skilled at managing your feelings and maintaining a rational perspective on the impact of someone else's behaviour, consequently choosing a more resourceful and measured response.

Moving beyond denial to acknowledgement

The next step to increased self-awareness is to acknowledge how you're feeling about a situation or person. Many pop psychology books talk about "Being positive" or "Getting in the zone". Unfortunately, if you're feeling very angry or sad, trying to be positive merely feels fake and inauthentic. Instead, I advocate simply acknowledging how you are feeling. This is not a negative approach that implies you will always feel this way, but a realistic view of how you are currently feeling.

It's useful to write down or quietly say to yourself: "I am feeling angry, disappointed, scared" or whatever applies. Sometimes the acknowledgement is all you need for those strong feelings to subside and become more manageable. One thing is for sure, feelings buried alive never die, and trying to suppress your emotions around a difficult issue will trip you up in your conversations. In my experience, when you don't acknowledge strong feelings they eventually leak out in your body language and tone of voice, hampering your best efforts at creating productive two-way dialogue.

 Key learn: Have your feelings or your feelings will have you.

Being okay with strong emotions

Some emotions feel very uncomfortable. For example, many people struggle to handle the feeling of loneliness and unconsciously use coping mechanisms like maintaining a hectic social life or always having a radio or television on so there's never a silent moment.

Uncomfortable emotions are there to act as signposts, informing you that you need to pay attention to something. When you consciously begin to sit with, rather than run away from, an unpleasant emotion, its intensity often diminishes as you acknowledge the signals it is sending out and begin to grasp what may be driving such a strong feeling.

Real-life case study: Finding the root emotion

I once sold a car privately to a buyer. About six weeks later, he called me to say that a fault had occurred with the gearbox and that he wanted a partial refund. I attempted to explain that the car was sold "as seen" and that I could not be sure how he had driven the car over the previous six weeks. The man became irate and after the call ended I became very angry as well. Even when I acknowledged the anger, it still burned red hot inside me.

I decided to sit with the anger and not to try to change it. After what seemed like a lifetime but was probably only two or three minutes, I realised that underneath the anger I was actually feeling scared. The man who'd bought the car was tall and muscular and although my ego didn't like to admit it, I was intimidated by his bulk and biceps! As soon as I acknowledged my fear and rationalised that this man wouldn't come back to remove one of my limbs, the anger drained away. Obviously I'd have preferred the man not to become irate, but by staying with the strong feelings, the true issue or in this case the sub-feeling came to the surface and I went from being unconsciously acted on by the emotion to identifying, acknowledging and working through it.

Mini exercise

The next time you experience an uncomfortable emotion, don't attempt to resolve it immediately, simply sit with it. Notice whether your relationship to the feeling changes over time or any insight or understanding pops into your thinking!

Top tip: Unpacking a jumble of strong feelings

Sometimes a vital conversation may be emotionally complex and you're likely to experience a smorgasbord of strong feelings that become entangled and confused. The resultant emotional overload can make it difficult to think the issues through with clarity and objectivity.

One way of separating out these various emotions is to use the metaphor of storage containers. You then allocate each feeling to the correct container. I use the following four vessels:

Container 1: Strong feelings I have about the other person.
Container 2: Strong feelings I have about the issues to be discussed.
Container 3: Strong feelings I have about actually having the conversation.
Container 4: Strong feelings I have about myself in the context of this situation/vital conversation.

For example, imagine you've had an argument with your partner or friend. The range of feelings you might be experiencing could include fear, resentment and sadness, and that's a lot to mentally process at one go. Let's say you use the containers and realise that you're resentful towards the other person because of the way they spoke to you, so that goes in Container 1. You drop your feeling of fear into Container 3, because you're afraid that the next conversation you need to have might raise deeper issues that you'd be uncomfortable adressing. Finally, your feeling of sadness goes in Container 4, as you are genuinely sad that you also used words that stimulated a lot of hurt in the other person.

There are two major benefits of dropping your feelings into specific containers:

❖ If the emotions stay intertwined, it's easy to be overwhelmed by the dominant emotion and lose a wider perspective. For example, if you focus solely on anger you may become obsessed with how the other person behaved, whereas if you pinpoint different emotions, the sadness you feel may encourage you to take more responsibility for your role in creating a destructive conversation.
❖ Although you are only writing the emotions down or mentally dropping them into the containers, doing so enables you to cognitively create some distance from and perspective on your emotions, making them easier to manage and work through.

The following questions may help you complete sections 2 and 3 of the vital conversations coaching tool:

❖ When you think about the person you will have the vital conversation with, what feelings do you have?
❖ How are you feeling about the issue(s) you need to discuss?
❖ Are there any aspects of the conversation that could create fear, anxiety or other strong emotions for you? Label them if you can.
❖ How are you feeling about yourself in the context of this conversation?

I would also like you to step into the shoes of the other person and literally become them. The way I recommend you do this is to physically stand or sit the way they would. Try to look out from their eyes, hear their voice and begin to hypothesize about:

* Any unresourceful feelings they might be holding around you or your behaviour or actions.
* How they feel about having this conversation.
* Any key issues or challenges for them that will raise strong emotions.

 Back to your VC coaching tool: Answer sections 2 and 3.

Developing compassion and empathy

By sorting through your own mix of emotions, you can begin to develop compassion for yourself, acknowledging just how difficult it can be to stay resourceful when challenging issues or circumstances arise.

If you took the time to reflect on how the other person was feeling, you may also have become increasingly aware of all the strong emotions that could be affecting them. You still may not appreciate the way the other person has behaved or the decisions they have made, yet by cultivating the early shoots of empathy for how they may be feeling, you can begin to see them as a human being who is also experiencing powerful emotions.

Further down the iceberg: Psychological needs

Everyone has physical needs that must be satisfied for basic survival, such as food, water, shelter, clothing and warmth. When

one of these physical needs is not met, it generates particularly uncomfortable feelings so that we take immediate action to resolve the problem. Beyond the physical dimension, we also begin to desire the fulfilment of needs that are more psychological in nature, yet these still have a tremendous impact on influencing how we feel and subsequently behave. (There's a list of psychological needs on page 85.)

When you engage in a vital conversation you are explicitly or implicitly communicating to the other person that you have unmet needs. For example, if the vital conversation is around your partner's repeated interruptions when you're trying to discuss important matters, you may have an unmet need for respect or fairness. If you want to talk to your boss about their micro management style, you might have an unmet need for more autonomy or trust. When you remain unaware of or don't acknowledge such core needs, it can be much more difficult to reconcile and work through the strong feelings you're having about what the other person has said or done. The dialogue you use in the conversation then tends to focus not on what you need but on what's wrong with the other person. You say to your partner: "You just don't listen. Why do you have to interrupt all the time?" This usually creates defensiveness. Alternatively, if you've recognised your unmet need for respect, you might say something like: "When you interrupt when I'm trying to share what's important to me, I get very frustrated. I would like you to have more respect for my point of view by allowing me to finish what I have to say."

Of course, it's possible that the other party might not agree with your observations about their behaviour. However, by sharing what's important to you at a deeper level and still taking ownership of your emotion ("I am feeling" rather than "You make me feel"), you increase the likelihood of productive dialogue in two ways. First, it's psychologically safer and therefore easier for the other person to hear your concerns without feeling criticised, thereby reducing defensiveness. Secondly, when you share how their actions have affected you at the level of core needs, the authenticity of your communication often generates empathy from the other party as they begin to hear in a non-judgemental way what's really important to you.

Case study: Underlying needs

Jane and Claire share a flat and have some differences around household chores.

JANE: Why do you have to keep leaving the kitchen like a pig sty? It's disgusting that I have to cook around all the old food you've left lying on plates. You need to start pulling your weight round here.

CLAIRE: Oh get over yourself, Jane, you're such a control freak. I have massive work commitments and the small amount of time I have for a social life and relaxation is more important than becoming an obsessive compulsive around cleaning.

You can see from this extract that the conversation is not going well, but what did you think were the underlying needs that were not being met for each person? You may find it helpful to look at the list of needs on page 85.

If I were mentoring Jane, I would be curious to find out if she had unmet needs around:

❖ Being understood (in the conversation itself)
❖ Support
❖ Cooperation
❖ Fairness

Claire's unmet needs might be:

❖ Autonomy/freedom (not being controlled by Jane)
❖ Understanding and respect (for her lifestyle choices)

Although you can make a hypothetical stab at what the other person's needs are, you can only truly acertain this when you talk to them. What you can do, however, is make sure that you've thought about which of your own needs have not been met, and how you can attempt to communicate those in a non-judgemental way.

Starting from needs increases the chances of a win/win outcome

Much has been written in business and management books about becoming solutions oriented, and there are certainly benefits of having this skill in your repertoire. The challenge comes when the other party doesn't want your solution. It's even more frustrating for you if you've invested significant time and energy developing that line of thinking. Until you know both parties' needs, your solutions or suggestions may miss the mark for the other person. In turn, their well-intentioned solutions may not work for you. Before long, you find that each party digs in their heels, championing their own view of how to take things forward.

 From a solutions-oriented approach, Jane may get pragmatic and suggest a cleaning rota or a policy of cleaning up after every meal. This is diametrically opposed to Claire's underlying need for autonomy and flexibility, and the idea is rejected. However, if they can share their needs with each other, they can begin to problem solve and design a solution that satisfies both.

For instance, possible solutions could be:

❖ They hire a cleaner.

❖ Claire eats more meals out.

❖ Jane outlines a level of cleanliness that she can live with and Claire can agree to.

❖ Claire suggests a level of commitment to cleaning she can adhere to and Jane is able to accept this and work around it.

❖ They agree that their personalities are not conducive to sharing a flat and one or both move out.

Understanding your needs and the other person's doesn't automatically mean that you will find an ideal way forward, but it will give you valuable insights into why you are having strong feelings about a situation or the person.

Back to your VC coaching tool: Answer section 4

Remember to take a look at the list of needs below. It may help you become more specific in pinpointing your own unmet needs.

Choice	Self-development	Being heard/seen
Liberty	Meaning	Belonging
Freedom	Purpose	Closeness/intimacy
Autonomy	Reflection	Sharing
Independence	Clarity	Trust
Individuality	Self-respect	Understanding
Self-empowerment	Self-worth	Emotional safety/
Solitude	Cooperation	freedom
Success	Consideration	Empathy
Excitement	Contribution	Equality/fairness
Passion	Reassurance	Friendship
Pleasure	Stability/reliability	Honesty
Fun	Support	Love
Relaxation	Acceptance	Predictability/
Authenticity	Affection	consistency
Creativity	Appreciation	Grieving

7
Story Time

"Reality is merely an illusion, albeit a very persistent one."
Albert Einstein

A s you read this chapter, I'm curious to know how you might feel and react if you were in this woman's shoes.

Real-life case study: Five cookies

A business woman has just made it through passport control and is looking forward to relaxing before her flight takes off. It's been a tough day, as two major client meetings did not go well and therefore she did not make the expected sales. She has around an hour before her flight leaves, so she buys a latte, her favourite magazine and a treat, a box of Millie's cookies. At around £6 for five these are expensive, but she feels she deserves a little luxury after the day she's had.

The airport is jam packed, but she finds a free seat and settles down at a small table, at which a Japanese man is already seated. With a relaxing sigh she begins to enjoy her magazine and coffee.

After approximately a minute she is rather alarmed to see the Japanese man help himself to one of her cookies. Although she is rather annoyed, she doesn't want to cause a scene, so she takes one for herself and gives the man a look of contempt.

The Japanese man smiles and then immediately takes another one.

Would you have said something by now? What would you have said?

The woman's initial surprise is turning to anger, her inner dialogue making remarks about this man that are unprintable! She removes another biscuit and munches it noisily, her eyes fixated on him. The Japanese man, not culturally accustomed to this much eye contact from a stranger, looks down and diverts his eyes, like a young child who's been naughty and is awaiting the inevitable parental reprimand.

A minute or two later, he reaches out to take the last cookie. Seeing his hand come across the table, the woman grabs the box. They both vie for the last cookie, the man's hand in the box and being pulled around the table by the business woman, knocking over her coffee and soaking her magazine. Finally, the man whips the final cookie from the box, quickly breaks it in half, slides one half across to the woman and pops the other half in his mouth. In a flying rage, the woman hurls the box at him and threatens to call security. Highly embarrassed, he mumbles an apology in broken English, bows and walks away.

How do you feel about the Japanese man's behaviour? Could you forgive him because he may not understand Western culture? Is it possible that he thought the cookies were being offered free by the airport?

I'll tell you the rest of the story later.

The power of a negative story

"Nothing is either good or bad but thinking makes it so."
William Shakespeare

Recall or imagine the following situation. You're driving down a motorway doing about 80 mph and you begin to notice that the car directly behind you is only 10 feet off your back bumper. There is a line of traffic in front of you, so no one is going to be able to go faster than the current flow of vehicles. Your first thoughts might be: "This is dangerous. That guy will never react in time if I have to break suddenly, he will go straight into the back of me." Your inner dialogue might then go something like this: "How irresponsible, what an asshole, how dare he put others' lives at risk?" If you are a parent, you might not even have your child in the car but that doesn't stop you from mentally turning the guy behind into a potential child murderer!

Your storytelling generates powerful emotions that are not confined to road rage. Have you ever caught your own inner voice saying things like:

❖ "He's such a control freak!"
❖ "What a drama queen!"
❖ "If she gives me that look one more time..."
❖ "What's his problem?"
❖ "I'm the innocent one in all this."
❖ "I'm such a doormat for accepting his/her bull.
❖ "This situation is beyond repair."

In this book I use the word "story" to represent your stream of thoughts about:

❖ The other person and their behaviour, actions or decisions.
❖ The conversation, relationship or issues.
❖ Yourself.

In this chapter you will see and experience that when your vital conversation involves high stakes, big consequences, differing opinions or relationship baggage, you have to remain incredibly vigilant about the stories you tell yourself – or pay the consequences in ineffective communication and damaged relationships.

Becoming hostage to your story

Below is an all too familiar scenario of how two reasonable human beings with good intentions begin to create a downward spiral that may eventually lead to a painful and costly break-up in their business and personal relationships.

Real-life case study: The ladder effect

John and Michael are business partners in a 20-person advertising agency. It's 9.15 a.m. and John is tapping his fingers on the desk, waiting for Michael to arrive so they can start their monthly meeting. This isn't the first time Michael's been late and John is fed up with his selfish approach. John believes that Michael's relaxed attitude towards time keeping does not respect his busy workload and sets a poor example for the office employees. When Michael arrives at 9.20 a.m. John greets him with a sarcastic comment about his need to invest in a more reliable alarm clock.

Michael is tired of John's digs. He became his own boss to get away from the 9-to-5 straitjacket and he's becoming increasingly frustrated that John's paranoia about time keeping is really disguising his need to control everything and be seen as the overall leader.

So how does someone end up turning a reasonable human being into an enemy? To answer this question you need to "unpack" how you create your stories.

Look at the diagram of the ladder of inference. Just below the first rung of the mental ladder is *directly observable data*. This is what you can see and hear as undisputable behaviour or facts. This level can be compared to what a camcorder would be able to record; that is, only what the parties did or said and not feelings, assumptions or judgements. In the case study, it's the time.

Ladder of inference adapted from *The Skilled Facilitator*, © Roger Schwarz 2002. Reproduced with permission of Jossey Bass, Inc.

At the next rung of the ladder, John *observes and selects data* to focus on: that Michael is not in the room and it's 15 minutes after the agreed meeting time. It's only when John goes up another ladder and *translates and labels* the data as "He's late" that the emerging story begins to create frustration and resentment.

Moving up a further rung, John now needs to *evaluate and mentally explain* Michael's absence. "Michael just isn't a team player. He obviously thinks it's OK to waste my time. Doesn't he realise he's setting a really poor example to the rest of the company?" Now John has made the mental leap to judgement and attributing motive to Michael's being late, which is currently an untested assumption. For instance, Michael may be stuck in traffic. At this point John also makes an unconscious switch from seeing the issue (Michael's lateness) as the problem to Michael the person being the problem! The story John is now hostage to will also be generating unmet psychological needs. At an unconscious level, his needs for respect and fairness are not being met, further magnifying his feelings of anger and frustration.

John has created what I would call an enemy image of Michael and only has to take the final step up the ladder where he *decides what kind of action to take.* John has been emotionally hijacked and his imminent future interaction with Michael will be heavily influenced by his story. John has decided that he is going to have to get tougher on Michael to make him more accountable. John will justify this path of action based on his good intentions to help Michael be more effective and create a professional image for the rest of the staff. However, it's highly unlikely that John will openly admit to Michael that he intends to manage him much more closely, so his decision making and thinking, and the reasoning that led to that decision, remain hidden, although Michael will undoubtedly notice the changes in John's behaviour.

Real-life case study: The ladder effect (cont.)

When Michael does enter the room, John is too wound up to notice that his business partner is looking pale and tired (observable data on the first rung of the ladder, because Michael's 1 year old kept both parents up most of the night). Instead, John finds a release for his pent-up emotion with a verbal side swipe: "When are you going to buy a more reliable alarm clock?"

In the blink of an eye, John has raced up his mental ladder. He has not yet developed the self-awareness to stop and question his story about Michael or his partner's motives for arriving late. Instead, he has made the fatal error of believing his assumptions about Michael's motives and behaviour to be true. If you believe something to be true, why would you question it?

A negative mind–body loop

You tend to go up the ladder of inference so fast that you believe your strong emotions are coming directly from what the other person did or said, when in reality your mental story is magnifying your emotional state. Once you're in this trap, it is very easy to believe that your response is justified. Let's face it, you're much more likely to let fly with a sarcastic comment if your story convinces you that the other person doesn't care about wasting your time than if you stay only with the observable data that for some unknown reason they are not in the room 15 minutes after the agreed time. Even if John doesn't let fly with a sarcastic remark, he will still be seething inside and that negative energy will leak out in his behaviour towards Michael.

Key learn

You think that all your emotion comes from what the other person has said or done, when in reality it's the story you create about what they have said or done that generates the majority of your strong feelings.

When your unchallenged story takes hold and you generate negative emotions, there are corresponding feelings and tension in your body. For instance, anger can create unpleasant bodily sensations in your stomach as well as excessive tension in your shoulders, jaw and other parts of the body. This unpleasant physical state sends messages back to the brain that all is not well.

When this also happens to the other person, unless they are self-aware they will not see that it is their own story causing this bodily stress. Hence they are likely to attribute their poor physical and emotional state unconsciously to what the other person has said and done. This reinforces or even enhances the story, leading to more emotion and tension, and so the cycle repeats itself.

Real-life case study: The ladder effect (cont.)

Returning to John and Michael, John's sarcastic remark kicks off a chain reaction that threatens to significantly damage their long-term ability to work together productively. It's now Michael's turn to race up his own ladder. The undisputable observable data is John's question, "When are you going to buy a more reliable alarm clock?" A quick succession of thoughts develops a story that allows Michael to cast John in the role of control freak. This is compounded by Michael's toddler-induced sleep deprivation, in his view a lack of empathy from John and his opinion that he has been unfairly judged. Instead of explaining why he's late, Michael throws John a look of contempt and decides (without sharing this with John) that he will resist all future attempts at what he sees as micro management. (Take a look at the diagram opposite to see the steps Michael takes up his ladder.)

From that moment on, John passes all Michael's behaviour, actions and results through the powerful filter that is his story about Michael's not being a team player. John begins to be overly specific about Michael's commitments, double checking his work, meeting times, agreed deadlines and so on. The filtering process becomes so biased that he misses the times when Michael demonstrates a very team-centred approach.

Key learn

You tell yourself a story and treat it as fact, act on it as if it were true and interpret everything else as evidence to support it.

Ladder of inference adapted from *The Skilled Facilitator*, © Roger Schwarz 2002. Reproduced with permission of Jossey Bass, Inc.

The cycle of destruction begins. John's decision to check on his partner's work gives Michael all the evidence he needs to prove that his business partner has indeed become a control freak. Michael reacts badly to this, becoming more elusive, defensive and demotivated. In turn, this behaviour gives John all the evidence he needs to convince himself that Michael really is selfish and is not a team player. The whole thing has become a self-fulfilling prophecy.

Within a few months their relationship has become so polarised that they find it hard even to be in the same room. What started out as different working styles and needs for work-life balance has become a bitter, antagonistic relationship. It's crazy to think that all this started with one person arriving 20 minutes late.

Mini exercise: Repeating your story creates amnesia
Think of someone you know whom you don't particularly like or find challenging to communicate with,

either at work or in your personal life. (Don't pick someone who has physically or emotionally abused you, as this exercise is not suitable for recalling such memories.)

Can you recall how you felt about them? What words would you use to describe them? In very specific terms, write down what they actually said or did that you didn't like.

If you came up with statements like "They were rude, distant, spoilt, domineering", then you are still talking about the other person from inside your story. When I run this exercise in my workshops, some delegates really struggle to identify specific negative behaviours or actions and can only recall the labels and judgements they assigned to this specific person. Those delegates then go on to realise that the enemy image or judgement labels that have placed on the other person are often very harsh compared to what the other person actually did or said.

In the case study above, John will not mentally run the story about Michael's lack of professionalism only once, he is likely to repeat it many times. While he's waiting for Michael to arrive he will be replaying it, and will probably do so again on the way home in the car, and perhaps even share it and the resultant feelings of frustration with his wife and close friends.

Each time you retell yourself a story, that story becomes the predominant memory and the facts become fainter and more distant, until only the story and its associated unresourceful feelings remain. This is why if you have a long-running issue with someone, you often lose touch with what they actually did and become fixated on who you believe they have become.

Collective storytelling

Sometimes people need extra support for their story, so they begin to bring in allies. The director of one business unit who has an enemy image of a fellow director starts to bad mouth that director's capability and decisions to the team he leads. Before long that group of people are all going up a collective ladder. His department slowly becomes more defensive and unhelpful to the other department, who in turn naturally start going up their team ladder. In a matter of weeks a silo mentality develops, where most of the focus of the two business units is on competing with each other and defending themselves, rather than uniting towards the key goal of being successful in their chosen marketplace.

A change in story changes everything

You can see from the diagram above that your stories lie at the bottom of your iceberg. In vital and difficult conversations they play the most significant role in affecting how you feel and subsequently how you behave towards and communicate with the other person.

Let's go back to the story about the cookies and the woman at the airport. She is livid: this man has helped himself to her precious biscuits, even when she has given him several signals to keep off! Anyway, she decides to run after this thief and give him a piece of her mind. She looks down to grab her bag, and as she does so, to her horror she sees her unopened, identical box of Millie's cookies...

How is she feeling now about the Japanese man? Well, once she has got over her shame, guilt and embarrassment, she probably has more positive feelings about him. More importantly, why has she just had such a rapid change in feelings? She has had a massive shift in the story she was telling herself. The story now probably goes something like: "Oh my God, he shared his box of biscuits with me. He gave me half of the last one even when I berated the poor chap and threw the box at him."

Perhaps you have had a similar shift in your story about this man. Do you now consider him to be kind, generous and compassionate to other people and their culture? If you did experience a shift in your story, you probably also had a shift in how you felt.

The change doesn't end there. If the woman thinks and feels differently, that may affect her behaviour. If she still decides to run after the man, she may apologise profusely, try to explain the misunderstanding and offer her biscuits as a way of saying sorry.

When you change your story, this produces change at every level. Even your deep psychological needs are changed if the story changes. This woman's need for respect and fairness quickly melted away when her villain story disintegrated.

The shifts in your story and the resultant changes in feelings may rarely be as dramatic as in the cookies story. Yet when you challenge your story and climb down your ladder of assumptions and judgements back to the facts, the perspective you can gain can be the difference that makes the difference in your ability to achieve real progress in your vital conversations.

For example, if John had asked Michael to share his reason for being 20 minutes late and Michael had explained that he had overslept because he had only had two hours' sleep, John might still have been frustrated, but it's highly likely that he would also have had a lot more empathy. More importantly, they might have talked about holding key meetings later in the day to factor in Michael's family situation.

Challenging your own mental story does not imply that you simply disregard the impact of the other person's behaviour or decisions. It's not about pretending that these don't matter. Becoming passive or silent would lead to frustration and the other party may repeat the unwanted behaviour. In my experience quite the opposite is true: if you don't communicate what's important to you, you find it very hard to drop your story and your negative emotions eventually cause havoc with either your relationship or your peace of mind.

In John's situation, this may not have been the first time Michael was late and it may well be that John should discuss the impact of Michael's behaviour in relation to meeting times. The big difference is that by challenging his thinking, John is no longer hostage to his story or his emotions and therefore he doesn't begin the self-sealing cycle of destruction with a sarcastic comment. John can now safely share his frustration with Michael, respectfully highlight the impact of Michael's behaviour, check out how Michael sees things, discuss a way forward and still maintain and even enhance the quality of their relationship.

Key learn

Different story = different needs = different feelings = different behaviour

Are you being thunk?

Here are three questions that begin to free you from your stories.

Are thoughts real?

From a physical perspective, thoughts are represented by a small electrical charge, so one could argue that they are real. Beyond this, however, they are just thoughts and they come and go. Have you ever considered just how many thoughts you have each day: hundreds, thousands? In the last chapter I explored how your thoughts can activate the hypothalamus in the brain, flooding the body with chemical messengers. These messengers can generate powerful emotions and strong physiological sensations that make your thoughts feel very real indeed.

Are thoughts facts?

Some thoughts are based on facts. If you're drinking a cup of tea and thinking how refreshing the tea is, that is a fact for you. If someone says the sun rises and sets each day, it would be easy to see this as a fact, although it is only a fact if you are viewing the sun set or rise from earth, since if you're out in space the sun shines continually. The challenge arises when you become attached to or, as Buddha said, "cling" to your thoughts and believe them to be facts.

Another way to look at this is to say that you begin to believe that the thoughts you are having are true and not, as they often are, untested hypotheses. In the first part of the cookies story, what were some of the "undisputed facts" or "truth" for the business woman (and maybe you)? He was eating her cookies! Was he rude, cheeky, a thief, culturally ignorant? These were just thoughts that her story turned into facts. The more she felt hurt, the more real her thinking became. In the second part of the cookie story she had a different set of thoughts about the man based on a new truth (they were *his* cookies), therefore the previous set of thoughts had to be just thoughts and not the truth.

Do you have to act on your thoughts?

You don't have to act on your thoughts, but if you fail to raise your self-awareness and challenge your stories, you often do act out your thinking. Had the business woman not paused to stuff the magazine into her bag before launching after the Japanese man, who knows what she would have acted out on him.

In reality, challenging your inner stories has far wider application and benefits than even your vital conversations. You can hold limiting assumptions and judgements around all aspects of your lives and the world in which you operate. To quote Salman Rushdie, "Those who do not have the power over the story that dominates their life, the power to retell it, rethink it, deconstruct it, joke about it, and change it as times change are truly powerless because they cannot think new thoughts." Therefore they cannot feel new feelings and subsequently cannot take new actions.

Key learn

With awareness you do not have to believe or react to your thoughts or story.

8
Managing Your Emotional State

"In the midst of winter I found within me an invincible summer."
Albert Camus

Having read Chapters 5 and 6 you have gained insight about the importance of enhancing your self-awareness, including the impact that unresourceful feelings and unmet needs can have on you. Chapter 7 considered how quickly a person can create emotionally charged stories that have a negative impact on their perception of and behaviour towards another person. Having built this core understanding, it's now time to learn and utilise specific emotional state management tools that will make a significant difference to your ability to engage in a vital conversation and remain resourceful.

Some tools will appeal to you more than others, but I would encourage you to have a child-like curiosity and to try out each tool at least once. Some may not work for you, but if you don't give them all a fair crack you may miss a valuable strategy for your vital conversations toolkit.

The mind–body connection

Have you ever had the experience of driving down a motorway on a long journey and beginning to be drowsy? Your body feels heavy and tired and your inner voice starts saying "I'm exhausted". The more you talk to yourself about being tired, the harder it becomes to keep your eyes open and you begin to slump. Unfortunately, as your body sags in your seat you feel even more fatigued, which repeats the cycle of "I'm tired" inner dialogue. Before long you have that nodding-off moment where you realise it's simply too dangerous to continue and you pull into a service station for a coffee. What's fascinating is that within 100 metres of walking from the car and changing to an upright walking position, you become significantly more awake and alert and probably wonder where your tiredness has vanished to. This example shows how the relationship between mind and body can have a powerful role in affecting your mood and mental agility.

I have explained how the mind, or more specifically the amygdala, can throw your body into a state of fight or flight without your conscious consent. Fortunately, you can also use your body to have the reverse effect on the mind, to calm it. Dr Herbert Benson devoted many years of study to the effects of deep and meditative breathing on the body. In his seminal book *The Relaxation Response*, he showed that deep diaphragmatic breathing switches the autonomic nervous system from a state of high alert and stress to a state of calm. This response lowers blood pressure and heart rate, relaxes the muscular system and increases the flow of blood to the brain's prefrontal cortex, giving us greater access to rational thought and better decision-making capabilities. In short, diaphragmatic breathing is an incredibly simple but effective tool for maintaining your composure.

Diaphragmatic breathing (breathing into the belly) is very natural to young children, but through repeated exposure to stress you become more and more conditioned to breathe into the upper chest, which unfortunately is anatomically hard wired into your stress-response mechanism and releases more adrenalin into the nervous system. Many people operate from a stressful state all the time because of their shallow rapid upper chest breathing.

You can benefit from diaphragmatic breathing in your vital conversations in two ways:

❖ The calming effect of diaphragmatic breathing decreases the possibility of the fight/flight response by reducing adrenalin and cortisol levels in the nervous system. This is critical just before you start the conversation, as this form of breathing reduces fear and nerves. Therefore you begin with maximum clarity and confidence.

❖ At any time in the conversation and often when you least suspect it, something may be said that throws you off balance. You can use diaphragmatic breathing to regain your composure and presence quickly.

Tool 1: Diaphragmatic breathing

As it's highly likely that you will be seated while having your vital conversation, while practising this technique sit in a straight-backed chair and make sure that both feet are flat on the floor. If possible, keep your spine straight but relaxed and close your eyes. Obviously, when you use this strategy in a vital conversation the other party will find it rather weird if you close your eyes for even a few seconds, but once you've become familiar with the process you can benefit from diaphragmatic breathing with your eyes open.

It helps to visualise a small deflated ball in your stomach. As you breathe in, visualise the air going deep down into your body, past the lungs and gently blowing up the deflated ball in your stomach for two to three seconds, until the ball is about 80% full. You don't want to over-inflate your lungs, as it's uncomfortable and has no further beneficial effect in this context. Hold your breath for two to three seconds and then very slowly release the breath again over a period of another two to three seconds. Repeat the process until you notice a more relaxed state in your body and a composed mind.

Here's the process again in step-by-step format:

1   Get into a comfortable position, seated with both feet placed on the floor, and keep upright with your eyes closed.

2. Visualise a deflated ball in your stomach. Breathe in very slowly through your nose and simultaneously visualise the air going into your stomach and inflating the ball.

3. Hold for two to three seconds (the time will vary based on your level of fitness and stress levels).

4. Very slowly breathe out. (Sometimes this is hard to do slowly through

your nose, so instead purse your lips as if holding a very thin straw and release the breath slowly, as if breathing out through the straw.)

5. Repeat until you sense your body relax and your mind become calm and increasingly rational.

Emergency first aid breathing

If you have lost your composure in a vital conversation and you're beginning to get stressed or, even worse, becoming emotionally hijacked, simply use diaphragmatic breathing as an anchor point for regaining your composure. Workshop delegates often say, "But if I focus on my breathing, I won't really be listening to what the other person is saying." My answer is that with practice you can go into this focused state of breathing and listen at the same time. If you get even close to becoming emotionally hijacked you will not be able to take in or process what they are saying anyway. You may as well stop listening for 10–15 seconds so that you can become mentally and emotionally effective again.

Dig the well before you need the water

Have you ever wondered why the army orders its soldiers to drill, drill and drill some more on key fighting skills? In the heat and pressure of battle, they understand that the soldier is much more likely to access his fighting skills if the response is habitual. In the same way, the diaphragmatic breathing technique needs to become a learned reflex. If you don't practise it on a regular basis then it is highly unlikely that you will remember or be able to access the technique when under pressure.

Simply for its stress-reducing health benefits alone, I recommend utilising diaphragmatic breathing several times each day. Repeating this breathing strategy on a regular basis will do wonders for your energy levels and peace of mind.

Take 30 seconds to practise diaphragmatic breathing when you:

❖ Wake up in the morning.
❖ Go to the loo.

❖ Stop to get a drink or a snack.

❖ Begin or end a car journey.

❖ Walk into your workplace or your home.

❖ Are in a lift or a queue.

If you incorporate this style of breathing into some of the activities above, the tool will become a habitual reflex in two weeks or less.

Tool 2: Combining breathing with acknowledgement

This is an especially useful technique if the other person in your vital conversation says or does something that triggers unresourceful emotions within you. The classic signs of a loss of mental composure are tension in the body, a shift to upper chest breathing and an increase in negative inner dialogue. When this occurs in a your vital conversation (and it will), use the following strategy:

1. Notice the strong feelings or physical tension in your body.
2. Acknowledge the strong feelings and if possible mentally label them ("I'm feeling frustrated", "I'm getting angry")
3. Breathe into your belly several times and induce the mental and physical relaxation response. If there are specific areas of tension in your body, try to relax these as you breathe out.
4. Check back in on your feelings and attempt to become a partially disassociated observer of them. For example, your disassociated internal dialogue might say: "Wow, that comment really has created some anger in me", rather than being lost in the anger (fully associated): "How dare you say that!"
5. Maintain slower, deeper breathing for a while until you feel that you have your composure back.

Key learn

Better breathing = better conversation

Watch out for don't statements

The mind is like a movie camera. Run a negative mental movie and negative is how you begin to feel. Switch to positive or more optimistic images and you gain access to more resourceful emotions and thinking.

Follow the instructions below:

❖ Don't think of the colour blue.
❖ Don't think of a pink elephant wearing a bowler hat.

What actually came to mind? Probably the colour blue followed by a secondary image of a rather strange-looking elephant. The mind does not easily compute "don't" statements. Instead, it creates the very picture or movie you didn't want to see. So as you're about to start your vital conversation, if your internal dialogue is saying "I really hope that I *don't* screw this up" or "I hope they *don't* lose it when I tell them such-and-such", you end up running that pessimistic video in your mind, which – hey presto! – kicks off a cycle of anxiety and tension in your body and voice.

Tool 3: Using visualisation and positive affirmation

You can use the power of visualisation to your advantage:

1. Well before the conversation takes place, find some private time when you won't be interrupted.
2. Calm your mind and body using diaphragmatic breathing.
3. Write down some statements about how you want the vital conversation to go. For example:
   "I will start with confidence and be clear about my reasons for the conversation."
   "I see both of us listening and finding a productive way forward."
   "I will be proud of myself for remaining calm and open, listening to their perception of the situation."
4. Close your eyes and visualise each statement for around 10-20 seconds. Allow the statements to create a video in your mind of the conversation being productive. You may see the other person responding

well to the way you listen, or you may begin to notice a feeling of confidence or courage as you see yourself being more assertive around an
important request that you want to make.

5. Repeat the visualisations two or three times and remember to acknowledge the positive/resourceful feelings that come from your thinking.

Visualisation on its own will not guarantee a smooth journey
through your vital conversation and should always be combined
with the thorough preparation I take you through in Chapter 9.
However, it has to help if you consider the positive effects it has
on your mind and your body.

Anchoring resourceful states

One way to have more choices about your emotional state is to
transfer resourceful emotions like confidence, calm and curiosity
from your past experiences via a technique known as anchoring.
You have been unconsciously using this strategy all your life.
Sometimes you create a positive anchor through repetition. You
may have a favourite piece of music that brings back a pleasant
feeling and every subsequent time it's played it strengthens the
association between the music and your emotional response.
Alternatively, a powerful anchor can be formed in one hit if the
experience had a significant amount of emotion linked to it.
Photographs of weddings, honeymoons and births are classic
examples of where pleasant feelings flow through you as you relive
the moment when you see the photo again.

Across your life you may have unknowingly developed some
anchors that automatically induce an unresourceful state. For
instance, if you had a significant relationship break-up or a bereave-
ment on a certain date, you may experience feelings of anger, sadness
or hurt again every year on that particular date. You can even have
negative emotional anchors to smells. Many people do not have the
best memories linked to the carbolic aroma associated with dentists.

You may also have picked up some unconscious anchors that may be particularly unproductive in a vital conversation. At an early age you may have witnessed or been on the receiving end of violent communication. You may have observed your parents having bitter and unproductive quarrels or been subjected to verbal bullying at some point in your career. All of these significant events have powerful negative emotions associated with them. The challenge comes when you experience similar situations in adulthood that trigger that anchor and generate fear, anger and other unwanted emotional states. These unconscious reactions tend to flip you into a first-generation, fight/flight mode. You may become passive and retreat into yourself, allowing further coercion or domination by the other party; alternatively you may go on the attack, as perhaps your role models used this as the best form of defence.

The important point to remember is that these unconscious anchors are just that, unconscious, and it helps to become more self-aware about how you trigger negative states in relation to conflict and potentially difficult conversations.

Real-life case study: Trapped in second-generation thinking

Carol was an only child. Not only had she witnessed her parents' persistent feuding, from her early teens she had been psychologically dragged into a triangular relationship where she often ended up as a mediator between her mother and her father. Witnessing her parents' fights was painful and unnerving, so she often found ways either to distract them or to de-escalate potential fights early by intervening and redirecting the conversation.

This continual vigilance developed a finely honed ability to read people and their moods swiftly and accurately. However, the scars of her upbringing also made Carol afraid of both conflict and emotionally charged situations.

Her ability to read people and adjust to their moods led her into a very successful career in sales, winning several awards in her company. She attended every sales course offered and even paid to attend several workshops on the latest in influencing skills. Unfortunately, most of this education was rooted in second-generation thinking, with an emphasis on how you sell your way of thinking to others.

When Carol's sales success catapulted her into management, she continued to use the same manipulative, second-generation approach that had produced such great results in the past. But managing and leading a team was far more involving and intimate than the hit-and-run sales relationships that were typical of that industry. Managing involved performance reviews and giving feedback. If a performance issue or conflict arose between her and the people she managed, Carol first attempted to coerce them with a second-generation approach, but when one of her team resisted or in her view become difficult, she found herself either attempting to caretake the situation by appeasing them, or shutting down the conversation and then avoiding the issue.

It was not until eight years later, after several unsuccessful attempts at management roles, that Carol realised that she had significant issues over conflict and strong emotions. Through counselling she began to identify her previously unconscious anchors and over time built new meanings around the benefits of healthy conflict and acknowledging the strong feelings on both sides. Today Carol is a successful manager and leader.

Mini exercise: Negative anchor awareness
Become more aware of any unresourceful negative anchors you may have by reflecting on your past career, significant relationships, schooling and childhood experiences. Think about the following questions:

❖ Have there been any people in your life who were poor role models of handling conflict or difficult conversations?
❖ Was it safe to communicate your needs or make requests of other people?
❖ Has there been a defining life moment or event that may have created a negative anchor around high-stakes conversations?
❖ Can you identify positive or negative relationship role models that may have shaped the way you now approach or avoid vital conversations?
❖ How do you communicate in high-stakes conversations? Is there any pattern of behaviour that might reveal a negative anchor?

Tool 5: Using anchors to your advantage

You can use anchors to your advantage by tapping into your positive memory banks and proactively anchoring the resourceful emotional states they invoke. You can then use this resource to emotionally support you through a challenging conversation.

This is how you do it:

1. Think of a resourceful state you would like to be able to access when you are engaged in your vital conversation. This could be confidence, compassion, courage and so on.
2. Remember a time in your life when you experienced that state, which doesn't have to relate to when you were communicating. Associate back into that moment: see what you saw, hear what you heard, feel what you felt. For example, if you want to access confidence you may remember a time when you were doing something that deep down you know you are really good at.
3. Once you have experienced that memory clearly and powerfully, access it again and this time when the feeling is at its strongest, create a physical anchor to that moment by squeezing your finger and thumb together on one hand. (You can use any part of your body to create the anchor, but I find fingers and thumbs practical and unobtrusive.) Doing so allows you to fire off the positive anchor at any time during a conversation without it being obvious to the other person.
4. Repeat the cycle of accessing the memory and physically anchoring the high point of the state until you can fire the positive state at will by simply squeezing your finger and thumb together.

If you want to build a bank of resourceful states for your vital conversation, simply anchor different states to different fingers. For example, there is nothing stopping you from pre-loading confidence, curiosity, compassion and clarity on each finger of your left hand. Just remember that you do need to repeat the anchor for each state several times to make it really effective.

The beauty of this strategy is that these resourceful states are now on tap. You can use them to get yourself into the right mental place before the conversation starts, and then if halfway through something is said that knocks you off balance, you can fire the anchor by squeezing the relevant finger–thumb combination and receive an immediate boost of that resourceful feeling.

Build these resourceful anchors well before you need them and practise using them in lower-stakes conversations first. As your confidence builds in your ability to access positive states at will, you can utilise the strategy in more challenging conversations.

Wisdom, compassion and courage

This strategy is not for everyone, but I find it valuable when I am engaging in really vital conversations and where it will be imperative for me to access all my courage, empathy and key conversational skills. This tool is most potent when used just prior to having your vital conversation.

Have you ever watched a film in which there was a character you really admired? You would love to be able to emulate some of the qualities they demonstrated in the movie: confidence, wisdom, eloquence, wit and so on. This strategy doesn't use Oscarwinning actors but three animals representing certain qualities that are highly supportive in your vital conversations.

In the picture below are three animals (I realize an owl is not an animal, but allow me a little poetic licence). Each is symbolic of particular characteristics, described below.

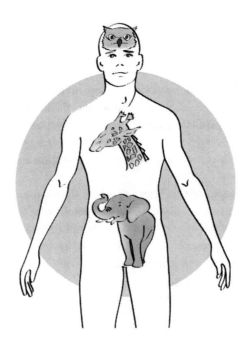

The owl

The owl watches from above, perched in your mind. It is a silent observer of both yourself and the other party. The owl is regarded as wise, skilful and a great listener, according to an often-quoted poem:

There was an old owl that lived in a oak.
The more he saw, the less he spoke.
The less he spoke, the more he heard.
Why are we not like that wise old bird?

The owl represents your ability to access your best communication skills and to view the interaction with perspective. The owl is also your internal observer, checking in and managing your emotional state and clarity of mind.

The giraffe

The giraffe has the biggest heart of any land-based mammal and in this tool resides in your chest area. The large heart metaphorically represents your ability to access compassion. When the other person is being argumentative or their emotions are getting the better of them, you can tap into the qualities of the heart. Even though you may not accept or take on board the other person's emotions or words, you endeavour to see beyond the behaviour and keep sight of the human being in front of you.

By holding this compassionate viewpoint, you also find it easier to be curious and have empathy for their viewpoint, situation and strong feelings. The more empathy and curiosity you have, the more the other person's barriers and fears begin to dissolve, broadening the communication channel between you and the possibility of a better outcome.

The big heart also signifies compassion for yourself. Sometimes you will be on the receiving end of bad news, feedback or behaviour that is hard to hear or accept. At these times you need enough compassion to acknowledge your feelings and give yourself some empathy in this challenging conversation.

The elephant

The elephant takes up residence around your belly button. It has enormous presence, is incredibly strong and will not be bullied by even the wildest animals in the jungle. The elephant visualisation is symbolic of generating the inner strength and resolve to see the conversation through and the courage to put forward your ideas and requests. Although you do not wish anyone any harm, when you access the elephant's qualities you will not be bullied and will lay down firm boundaries on behaviour that is unacceptable.

Each animal also enables the others to maintain their strengths. For example, the giraffe's big heart makes sure that your elephant doesn't become overly confident and go on its own bullying stampede. The wise owl makes sure that the giraffe doesn't become overly vunerable about displaying emotions if the person in front of you is likely take advantage of your honesty.

Tool 6: Coordinating your inner power animals

1. Find a place where you won't be disturbed, get comfortable in a chair, plant your feet firmly on the ground and close your eyes.
2. Visualise the owl, giraffe and elephant being located in your body at the various points shown in the diagram.
3. Do some diaphragmatic breating, as in Tool 1. On the in breath imagine the air going from your stomach past the elephant then up your spine, passing through the giraffe before ending up at the owl (at the crown of your head).
4. On the out breath, visualise the air going from the owl down the front of your body through the giraffe and passing through the elephant and down to your belly button.
5. Maintain this cycle of breathing in and out with the visualisation for between five and nine cycles, or until you start to get comfortable with breathing and keeping the visualisation in your mind's eye.
6. Allow the breathing and visualisation to connect you to the qualities or characteristics that the animals represent. See yourself taking on and utilising these attributes in your vital conversation.

7. Practise this technique several times until you find it easy to hold the visualisation in your mind while completing the breathing cycle.

8. Use this tool for a couple of minutes before your vital conversation to connect with the qualities and characteristics that will support you through your conversation.

Feel free to change the symbols you visualise. The animals chosen here work for me, but you may have different symbols that are more meaningful for you.

Tool 7: See them beautiful

Marshall Rosenberg has used his mediation skills and non-violent communication process to broker peace and understanding in conflicts from the Middle East to Africa. He brings violently opposed people together and eventually, through his skill and unwavering empathy and compassion, gets each side to recognise the human being across the table. Marshall calls this "seeing them beautiful".

He would be the first to admit that it's not always easy to see the other person as beautiful, especially if they have hurt, frustrated or disappointed us in some way. He has many ways to convey his message and often uses songs, of which the following is an example reproduced with the permission of the original artist:

See me beautiful,
Look for the best in me,
That's who I really am,
All I ever want to be,
It make take some time,
It may be hard to find,
But see me beautiful.

See me beautiful,
Each and every day,
Could take a chance,
Could you find the way,
To see me shining through,
In everything I do,
And see me beautiful.

"See Me Beautiful" from the recording *Teaching Peace*, © 1986 Smilin' Atcha Music. Written by Red and Kathy Grammer. Distributed through Red Note Records, www.redgrammer.com.

Both in my personal life and before a highly charged mediation, I silently sing this song to myself to create a feeling of compassion and empathy. When my son is having a "test dad's boundaries day", singing this song helps me to reconnect with just how incredible he is and with the truth that he is being at his best by just being himself. That for me is beautiful.

Part III
Preparation

9
Preparing for Your Vital Conversation

"Do your own thinking independently. Be the chess player, not the chess piece."
                                                              Ralph Charell

Now that you've decided who you need to have a vital conversation with and you have mastered your emotions, you can't just steamroller ahead and begin to talk. To get the result you want, you need to plan and prepare. But when you begin to plan your vital conversation, the chances are that your mind will be full of different thoughts, fears, hopes and feelings. It can take all your mental processing power simply to gain a clear perspective on the people and the issues involved, let alone imagine how you will actually engage in the conversation.

Opposite is a pictorial view of what might be buzzing through your mind as you begin to contemplate your vital conversation.

As a coach and mediator, I have had the privilege of observing and facilitating other people's thinking during high-stress conversations. This unique and detached vantage point has enabled me to unpack that jumbled thinking into distinct areas. In this chapter I help you unpack your own thinking by analysing the key steps you need to take in your preparation. It's quite a long chapter, but use the vital conversations coaching tool step by step and it will give you unique insights, increased clarity of purpose and a solid foundation from which to begin your vital conversation.

Walking in another man's moccasins

An ancient American Indian saying goes: "Don't judge another before first walking a mile in the other man's moccasins." Being able to step into another person's shoes and see the world from their perspective isn't easy. If you're holding a negative opinion of the other person or their actions, you may be too angry or frustrated to access the compassion or curiosity you need to suspend your own point of view, even temporarily.

However, I do encourage you to build your approach to your vital conversation based on both parties' perspectives. Of course, until you get to the actual conversation any attempts you make to understand the other viewpoint must by definition be only your hypotheses of what might be going on.

Nevertheless, your investment in seeing another person's universe from "second position" has long-term benefits. You often realise that they are experiencing strong emotions, fears and uncertainty, just as you are, and this alone can shift your stance from having an image of them as obstinate, rude or controlling to seeing them as a human being once more.

Step 1: Capturing your story's headlines

You have already seen how your own unchallenged stories about your vital conversation and the associated relationship can create havoc in your mind, generating powerful emotions and seriously undermining your ability to gain a rational perspective. To have any chance of creating a safe and productive dialogue, you must first take control of your story, becoming master rather than servant.

Think about the vital conversation that you need or want to have. Think about the person you will have the conversation with. Think about the issues at stake and the potential consequences. Can you identify any unhelpful stories that you're constructing?

Sensational headlines sell newspapers: "UK economy in ruins!" "New super virus could kill millions!" Even though they are often generalisations or largely inaccurate, they succeed in grabbing your attention. Their doom-and-disaster nature often creates enough tension, excitement or fear that you buy the paper.

When your career, goals or personal relationships are being negatively affected by someone else, you tend to write dramatic mental headlines about it, like "He's deliberately turning the kids against me!" or "She's ruining my credibility!" These headlines may be partly factual – your ex-husband may be indeed saying negative things to the children about you – but do you really want the story to take you over? Will you really make any progress with the other person's behaviour if you continue to allow your story to emotionally hijack you?

Have you been guilty of crafting any of these headlines about someone else?

- ❖ She's so irresponsible.
- ❖ They just can't be trusted.
- ❖ She's incapable of love, honesty, appreciation.
- ❖ It's like talking to a brick wall.
- ❖ He's suffocating me.

❖ He has no appreciation for the pressure I'm under.
❖ She's trying to make me look like a fool.
❖ They're too stupid to get my ideas.

Or any of these headlines about a situation, an issue or a potential consequence?

❖ If we don't get this project back on track I will lose all credibility with my boss.
❖ Having a conversation will only make this go from bad to worse.
❖ If he doesn't go to college my son will end up serving burgers for the rest of his life.
❖ Their dog's persistent barking is making my life a misery.
❖ If they want a fight they'll get one.
❖ It's going to tear our relationship apart.

My strategy is to poke a little fun at this kind of tabloid sensationalism, using light-heartedness to gain some perspective on a story that may be getting out of control.

Mini exercise
Take a moment to consider the issues that are relevant to one of your future vital conversations and write down any headlines that your mental story creates about the person involved, the situation or yourself. To create more drama and fun, write the headlines out in large letters – with an exclamation mark if you feel like really going for it.

My wife is turning the children against me!

They are totally unprofessional!

She's trying to destroy my credibility!

He's a total control freak!

I'm a complete doormat!

Although this may seem like an over-the-top exercise, it can help you become aware of how your story has twisted the facts. This in turn helps you regain control and perspective, reducing the emotional volatility that an unchallenged story may provoke.

Step 2: Climb back down your ladder

On page 89 I describe a model called the ladder of inference, which highlights how you can go from the bottom of the ladder (observable facts/hard data) to the top of the ladder (your story) in a matter of seconds. It's time to start climbing back down your ladder and return to the facts of the situation. When you get round to having your vital conversation, explaining how you see things from the bottom of the ladder will significantly reduce the potential for defensiveness in the other person, as they will be more ready to hear your version of events, if you have stripped your story of judgements, labels and generalisations.

Answer the following questions based on the vital conversation you have chosen. To give you some direction, I've added example answers based on a working scenario that is not unusual. Jim is a management consultant and a member of a team working on a big client implementation project. In team meetings one of his peers, Caroline, has a communication style that really winds him up.

To get the full benefit from this exercise, answer the questions based on the unchallenged story you have been telling yourself for your vital conversation, including any judgements, labels, generalisations, negative characterisations or strong feelings – even the odd rude word is acceptable!

1. Up to now, what has been your story about the other person involved in your vital conversation?

e.g. *JIM: The woman's a control freak, she hogs the air time and aggressively puts down other people and their point of view.*

2. What's your story about the key issues?

e.g. *JIM: Other team members are afraid to speak up and it's destroying the team's confidence, morale and creativity.*

3. What's your story about yourself and your role in this situation?

e.g. *JIM: It's not my responsibility to sort this out. Our team leader should be addressing this outrageous behaviour.*

Now it's time to climb back down your ladder. Can you be sure that your story is 100% factually accurate and free of any assumptions, generalisations, labels or bias? Circle the appropriate answers below.

1. Your story about the other person and their role is 100% factual.   Yes/No

If your answer is no, climb back down your ladder and describe the behaviours or facts of which you can be absolutely sure:

JIM: On three occasions she's raised her voice, pointed her finger and challenged people using comments like "That's never going to work".

2. Your story about the issues is 100% factual.   Yes/No

If your answer is no, climb back down your ladder and describe the behaviours or facts of which you can be absolutely sure:

JIM: Other team members rarely add suggestions, but I haven't actually asked them if this is directly related to Caroline's behaviour. If I'm honest, I only know that I am intimidated by Caroline's style.

3. Your story about your role in this situation is 100% factual.
Yes/No

If your answer is no, climb back down your ladder and describe the behaviours or facts of which you can be absolutely sure:

JIM: I have made negative comments about Caroline's behaviour to other team members. Caroline and I are the same grade and if I have a problem with her style or behaviour, it would make sense for me to discuss this with her directly.

Key learn: Let go!

It's not always easy to let go of a story that allows you to feel victimised or morally superior, or that conveniently masks our contribution to the issues. However, removing the fog that is your biased story can allow you to approach your vital conversation with clarity and honesty.

Back to your VC coaching tool: Answer section 5.

Step 3: Identify your baggage

From early childhood you are exposed to a multitude of experiences. Some may have been painful events, like witnessing a parental separation or the impact of being bullied. Your perceptions and beliefs about others can also be heavily influenced by what you are told or guided into thinking. Having seen many war films as a young lad, I remember believing that Germans were dangerous and aggressive people. Even in my teens I still perceived that country as having the potential to start another war if it got the chance! It was only when I was 19 and I took the opportunity to study in Germany for three months that I realised this was a nation that believed in peace and democracy, and that it was incredibly sad about its past contribution to wars that had killed so many innocent lives.

Even in our so-called civilised society, historical baggage is still colouring the perceptions of millions of people and consequently having a negative impact on how they interrelate, from religious hatred to discrimination based on ethnicity, sexual orientation, age, gender, disability or social stereotypes.

It can be very painful to admit to yourself that you have accumulated baggage or developed some form of bias about someone, and yet if you are to be truly effective in your vital conversation, you have to be ruthless about acknowledging that bias.

Once again, it can be useful to look at your story about the person with whom you're planning to have a vital conversation. Sometimes the baggage has become so ingrained in your day-to-day thinking that you don't realise you're projecting your bias. You may think things like "Well, you know how emotional women can get" or "The reason he acts that way is that he suffers from small man's disease" or "Ultimately as a mother she's always going to be more committed to her children than to this team". If you don't acknowledge and let go of such slanted views, they will infect your behaviour and therefore the responses you receive from other people.

The history of the relationship

"Resentment is like drinking poison and then waiting for the other person to die."   Carrie Fisher

One of the most obvious areas of baggage about which you need to remain vigilant is how the history of a particular relationship affects your perceptions and your decision making. For example, if as a child your mother repeatedly threw you a guilt trip about being ungrateful, as an adult you may find it incredibly challenging to make requests or share your disappointment about another person's behaviour or actions. At work you may have previously had several awkward conversations with a colleague who was not hitting deadlines on a key project. Six months and an organisational reshuffle later, you are now that person's boss and you have to give them their first performance review. Could you keep your previous angst from influencing their grade?

I'm not saying that you should necessarily forgive, forget or move on from someone's previous misdemeanours; the reality is that you could still be hurting, angry or grieving from what the other person said or did. The key here is self-awareness. Acknowledging your baggage and working through it can be a conversation maker or breaker. Free from bias, your original motive for the conversation that was soaked in revenge or blame shifts to a more authentic intention focused on facts, feelings, behaviours and impacts.

If at all possible, try to put the issue you want to raise and the history of your previous interactions into separate compartments. Once again, acknowledge any strong feelings and then challenge yourself to stay with merely the facts about this particular situation. This isn't easy to do, and yet if you don't and your historical baggage takes control, the chances are that the toxicity will leak out and derail your vital conversation.

If you really cannot let go of or accept the past, it does beg the question of whether your first vital conversation needs to focus on clearing up previous issues and bad feeling.

Haunting conversations

Rather than baggage about a particular person, you may be carrying baggage concerning a specific type of conversation. You may need to end a significant relationship and yet you feel paralysed because of your experience of a very similar conversation with a different partner several years before. That conversation quickly became an emotional tsunami that evolved into a bitter and protracted break-up, from which you took months to recover.

What's important here is to remember that then and now are different. It may be worth looking back to understand what might have contributed to the conversation's downfall, but at the same time you now have this book and an increasing self-awareness that should give you a much better shot at achieving a favourable outcome.

Seeking professional help

On a serious note, you may have been subjected to physical, emotional or sexual abuse or may have been through a particularly dark time in your life. Significant negative life events can create deep-seated beliefs about people and the world. Experiencing infidelity from someone you thought you would be spending the rest of your life with may create a generalised belief that no one can be trusted, which will undoubtedly affect all significant conversations you have or avoid with future partners. If you believe that you have been deeply affected by a life event or another person, I would recommend you seek professional advice and support.

Real-life case study: Projected baggage

David eventually shared with his wife Helen that as a child he had been repeatedly sexually abused by a doctor during a two-week stay at the local hospital. Helen felt incredibly sad for David and angry at the doctor, who had committed suicide when the abuse had been revealed in the local press some 20 years previously.

From time to time Helen had to visit the same hospital to sort out some problems with their toddler. A few weeks after the conversation with David, she became aware that she was being increasingly short-tempered with the hospital staff. It was then she realised that she was still carrying anger about what had been done to David and was projecting that anger on anyone working at the hospital. Most of them wouldn't have known the doctor concerned, let alone had anything to do with the abuse.

Once she had realised this, Helen was able to recognise her projected anger and adjust her behaviour towards those working in the hospital. Sometimes self-acknowledgement is all that's required to let go.

Back to your VC coaching tool: Answer section 6.

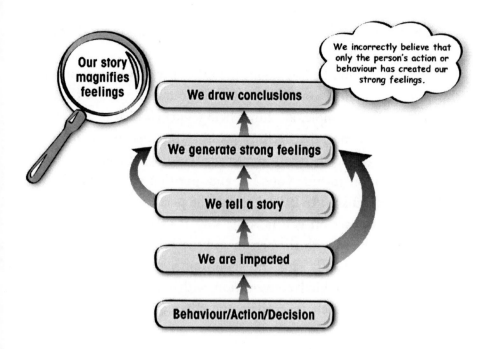

Step 4: Intentions – Understanding the action-impact-intention trap

The figure above is a quick recap on how your story affects your perception of events. In essence, someone does or says something that has a negative impact on you. You tell a story that magnifies how you feel about what's happened, which in turn influences the conclusions you draw, the subsequent actions you take and the impressions you create about the other person.

This journey from the initial impact to drawing conclusions has only taken a few seconds at most. Within that time frame you get hit with a burst of negative emotion and adrenalin that surges through your body and cuts off half your brain power. In this stressed state of mind, you make the very natural mistake of believing that all your emotions were a result of the other person's actions. What you don't realise is that you haven't acknowledged the part your own story making has played in amplifying such a negative reaction. It's in these supercharged story moments that you begin to question the other person's intentions and you fall into the action–impact–intention trap.

What you believe about the other person's intentions has a powerful influence over how you feel about and relate to the other person. For example, all things being equal, which person would create more negative feelings within you: Person A, who did something that hurt you, or Person B, who did something with the intention to hurt you? I'm guessing that you picked B. The moment you shift to believing that the person intended to have a negative impact on you in some way, it gets personal. Now you have a problem with the person and their character, not just with the issues at hand. This will significantly reduce your ability to engage in your vital conversation with empathy, curiosity and compassion, which are cornerstone values of the third-generation mindset.

Charity begins at home

Lee Ross, a professor of social psychology at Stanford University, coined the term "fundamental attribution error". The theory is that when you try to explain other people's behaviour, you tend to overestimate the role of personal factors. You interpret someone else's actions in terms of your view of the person's character (lazy, forgetful, unprofessional, greedy and so on). Such an interpretation underestimates or ignores the impact that the external environment or situational factors has had on the person's actions.

In contrast, when you are placed in a difficult situation or you make a mistake, the tendency is to be far more forgiving of your own intenrions and character and much more inclined to blame situational factors. This makes perfect sense, as you know better than anyone what external factors have been influencing your behaviour and decisions. When someone else affects you, it is their behaviour that is most obvious to you, not the hidden situational factors that might be influencing them. If you pick up a parking ticket because you ran over on the meter, you were overloaded with errands, whereas if your partner gets a ticket they are absent minded and don't care about wasting the family finances. Have you ever noticed that when you're driving down the motorway, the person going 20 mph slower than you is an idiot and the person driving 20 mph quicker is a maniac, yet you are obviously driving at the "right" speed!

The key here is to step back from your story and ask yourself "Why would a reasonable human being have acted this way?" or "What external factors could be at play here that have led to this behaviour or action?" I'm not saying that people don't sometimes have bad or complex motives, because they clearly do. I'm also not saying that you should try to invent a number of Pollyanna reasons that diminish the other person's responsibility for how they have behaved. However, when you can step back from the intention trap and look for external mitigating factors, you may reach a more rational perspective and focus on trying to understand *why* this person did what they did rather than creating an enemy image.

Key learn

You see your own behaviour and intentions in a much more favourable light than the other person's.

Case study: Consequences of the action-impact-intention trap

Henry and his partner Judith are having friends over for dinner. It's 7.30 p.m. and while keeping an eye on the meal, Judith has repeatedly asked their 8-year-old son Marcus to get ready for bed. Marcus is running round the house overtired and not following his mum's wishes. Henry and a male guest who arrived early are glued to the television, catching up on the day's football results.

In a moment of exasperation, Judith storms into the lounge and says, "For God's sake, Henry, can you get off your backside and get Marcus off to bed?" Henry is taken aback by her frustration and follows her into the kitchen. They have the following conversation:

HENRY: What's with embarrassing me in front of Michael?

JUDITH: Henry, I'm not trying to embarrass you, but you must be blind if you can't see that it's way past Marcus's bedtime and I'm trying to get dinner ready for eight people.

HENRY: Why do you have to get in such a state? Sometimes I think you just do it for the drama.

JUDITH: How dare you say that? I'm trying to make this a special evening. You just don't see the effort I put in, it's like you take it all for granted.

HENRY: I work hard all week, I watch 20 minutes of football and you're trying to make me feel guilty.

How do you feel when you're accused of having bad intentions? When Henry says "What's with embarrassing me in front of Michael?" what he's not directly saying but still implying is "You intended to embarrass me". Is Judith likely to agree with that diagnosis? To agree, she would have to concede that she wants to publically shame the person she loves the most. When accused of bad intentions, the vast majority of people defend their behaviour, as the alternative is to admit to a character flaw that is usually diametrically opposed to how they view themselves.

You can get so lost in defending yourself against the accusation of negative intentions that you spiral into two further conversational black holes. First, you retaliate by accusing the other person of negative intentions in their turn. This leads to tit-for-tat trench warfare, where no progress is made but there are significant casualties on both sides. Alternatively, you may react as Judith did and say something to the effect of "I didn't intend to embarrass you". Having explained your true intention, you somehow believe that once you've said you didn't mean to hurt, offend or embarrass the other person, the impact of your actions has been erased. In the rush to defend your intentions and character, you become blind to the fact that the other person is still hurting from what you've said or done, whether that be real or perceived.

If you practise third-generation thinking, as described in Chapter 4, when you are accused of bad intentions you breathe deeply and acknowledge your feeling of defensiveness. Having regained your emotional composure, you attempt to create a more compassionate focus. Seeing beyond the other person's accusative tone, you ask yourself: "How are they hurting and what do they need?" It's not about condemning your own character, but it is about realising that if the other person does not get some acknowledgement of how they are feeling, the conversation could quickly degenerate. It's also about having the courage to say sorry if your initial words warrant an apology.

This is how Judith may have reworded her response if she was able to come from a third-generation mindset:

"Henry, although I didn't intend to embarrass you, I can see how what I said did, and I'm sorry. It's just I really need your support right now, and when you didn't help out with Marcus I became angry. Right now we have dinner guests arriving, but perhaps tomorrow we could talk about my need for more support in these situations. How does that sound to you?"

Getting a better perspective on intentions

When you find yourself thinking that the other person has bad intentions, use the following six-step process:

1. Breathe (take diaphragmatic breaths and get into a rational state)
2. Impact (what was the actual impact on me of their behaviour/action?)
3. Story (what story have I been telling myself to accuse them of bad intentions?)
4. Facts (what did they actually do, specifically?)
5. Reason (why would a reasonable human being have acted this way?)
6. Influence (are there any external situation factors that could have influenced their behaviour?)

Using these six steps can help to take the emotional volatility out of the other person's negative impact. From this space you also have a more rational perspective and hypothesis on the other person's intentions.

Ruthlessly interrogate your own intentions

"One may as well start with the truth as one will end up with the truth."
Earl Shoaf

When you're preparing for a vital conversation, you need to have a thorough understanding of your own intentions in relation to the other person. But you can't do this without honest self-reflection. You have to challenge yourself to question whether you have any suspect motives. Vital conversations are not usually straightforward and it is possible to have dubious intentions behind what you say and want to achieve. For example, did Judith actually want to embarrass Henry in front of one of their guests? Perhaps deep down she believes that shaming Henry is the best way of motivating him to be more supportive.

Sometimes it isn't fair to describe your intentions as dubious, but they may well be complex. For instance, if you agreed to take your daughter to gym club but failed to get home in time because you allowed your work commitments to overrun, you hopefully didn't intend to hurt your daughter's feelings, but you did care more about your work that day.

Digging down to the truth of your core intentions can be quite disconcerting. You may have to take a long, hard look in the mirror and have the courage to admit to yourself that you have questionable or complex intentions.

Real-life case study: The best of intentions?

Tim, a successful IT consultant, is also a volunteer coach for a very successful under-12s football team. While attending one of my workshops, he decided to prepare for a vital conversation with the parents of one member of the team, who was underperforming. The boy was spending most of the game either making mistakes or being a substitute. Tim wanted to talk to his parents about transferring the boy out of his squad and into a less competitive league. He believed he was operating from the best of intentions: he didn't want the boy to lose confidence and he didn't think it was fun for him to spend lots of time on the bench. These intentions were going to be the foundation of his conversation with the parents.

I asked Tim to search his soul for any complex or dubious intentions. Later that day, he revealed to the group that actually the truth was that he was hypercompetitive and the boy was a weak link in an otherwise highly talented squad. Tim desperately wanted to win the league that year and his primary motive was to bring in a stronger player to maximise his chances. The other intentions were still valid, but he had taken an honest look in the mirror and consequently redesigned his approach to be more transparent about both the boy's interests and his own aspirations for the team.

Imagine if Tim had decided not to share his motive of only wanting players who are good enough to win the league. If he only focuses on the intention that he doesn't want to see the boy's confidence eroded, where does he go with the conversation if the boy's parents and the lad himself still want him to play? He's then painted himself into a corner. He could back down and keep the boy on the team, but he would be undermining his own ambitions. He could raise the stakes and tell the parents that they should care more for the boy's long-term confidence, but that would be duplicitous. Finally, he could admit his true intentions about wanting success for the team, but the parents might very well feel deceived by his earlier solitary focus on their child's interests.

In the short term it is definitely more challenging to be transparent; you may not feel confident being so honest about your own interests and intentions. There is also a high probability that your willingness to be transparent will invite tougher scrutiny from the other person and that will make the conversation more challenging. In my experience, however, the truth about either party's intentions will surface at some point. It may not happen in the conversation itself, but it will inevitably play out in the ongoing personal or working relationship. The other person may not always like you when you are this transparent about your intentions, but doing so will develop increasing levels of trust and respect, which are the hallmarks of a quality relationship.

Back to your VC coaching tool: Answer sections 7-10

Step 5: Letting go of the blame game

At times of stress, conflicting viewpoints and high-stakes issues, apportioning blame comes very naturally to the human psyche. Take the credit crunch: in researching blame on Google I came across no fewer than 300 articles where the headline had something to do with "Who's to blame for the credit crunch?" Everyone seems to be blaming everyone else.

Blame is ingrained from an early age. Taking the blame at home or at school usually led to unpleasant consequences. It meant admitting that you were wrong, bad or incompetent in some way, which did wonders for your self-esteem. But by far the most disconcerting aspect of being on the wrong end of the blame stick was the likelihood of punishment: being grounded, school detention or even physical pain. Chastisement could also be intangible, in the form of moralistic judgements, being shamed or ignored. Is it any wonder that wherever possible you fought tooth and nail to prove your innocence by either denying your involvement, counter blaming or deflecting the problem onto someone else? "I didn't break the window, Mrs Hunter, it was Johnny, he made me throw the ball!"

The pros and cons of blame

Above and beyond the obvious benefit of not being punished, blaming someone else can feel particularly cathartic. This person's behaviour or decisions have affected you and it's an opportunity to download your tension and negative emotion onto them. As an added bonus, if you can create a story of how you have been the victim and the other person has been the villain, you can generate enough blame to mask any contribution you may have made to the situation.

However, the downsides of blame are numerous and can be costly. First, blame creates defensiveness. If you don't like being blamed you can hardly castigate the other person for feeling the same way. If you default to blame, the likely outcome is that they will fight their corner or throw the blame firmly back in your lap. Even if you have the trump blaming card and the case appears to be open and shut, there are further serious drawbacks to operating from a blame mindset.

Case study: Brotherly love

Ted is the father of 18-year-old Jake and 16-year-old Simon. They boys have been to a mutual friend's 18th birthday party and at 1 a.m. Jake has to try to get Simon up the staircase and into bed. Simon has drunk more than he can handle and wakes the rest of the house up as he distributes the contents of his stomach over the landing carpet.

The next day Ted launches into an attack on their immaturity and lack of consideration and responsibility. He's especially hard on Jake. Jake attempts to defend himself, but his father gives him a guilt trip about not looking after his younger brother. Simon is grounded for two weeks and Jake is given the "look" and silent treatment for the rest of the weekend.

Three months later, Jake and Simon are out and Simon has overdone the drinking once more. Does Jake do the right thing and take his brother back to the safety of their home, or does he avoid the blame and decide that he's not going to take the rap for his brother's drinking and leave his semi-conscious brother to his own devices?

The defensiveness that blame causes usually only allows for a surface-level diagnosis of the underlying problems. A second consequence is that people who are blamed usually do their best not only to hide future recurrences of that specific problem but also new mistakes. Blame kills honesty and collaboration, and its ramifications can be far reaching and serious.

Become a systems thinker

Systems thinking originated in engineering in the 1940s, although its application to human communication and organisations really only came into existence in the 1960s. It represents a unique approach to problem solving, as it views the problem as part of an overall system. In relation to the credit crunch, it's easy to see why the finger of blame was pointed in so many directions: hedge fund managers, central banks, governments. In reality, however, it was a catastrophic failure of the whole system, with many interrelated contributions.

From the viewpoint of blame, it's easy for Ted to pass judgement on the boys. Simon has demonstrated his immaturity by drinking too much. Jake has shown a lack of responsibility, in Ted's opinion, by not stopping his younger brother from over-doing it. If we take a systemic view of the problem that Ted and his sons face, what other inputs are involved? Perhaps the parents have not invested enough time in understanding why Simon drinks himself unconscious. Are there issues at home or external influences from peers that have had a bearing on his relationship to alcohol? How much should Jake be accountable for? Does he have the maturity and skills to be taking care of his younger brother in these situations and is it reasonable to burden him with that responsibility?

Think inputs!

When you think in a systemic way, you ask yourself about the different inputs to the issues you wish to discuss in your vital conversation. If you succeed in letting go of blame, you can break the possible inputs down into four areas:

* How do I input to this issue? (What did I do/not do?)
* How does the other person input? (What did they do/not do?)
* Did anybody else have an input?
* Are there any non-human external factors to be considered?

Your input to an issue is often greater than you may realise. As French dramatist Molière said, "It is not only what we do, but also what we do not do, for which we are accountable."

For example, when employees complain among themselves

and blame management for the current state of the company, they often add to the problem by withholding the very feedback that may influence or improve senior management's decision making. If you walk down a dark quiet alley late at night and are mugged, you obviously didn't purposely walk down there to be relieved of your personal possessions, but (while I'm not condoning this type of crime) you did contribute to the likelihood of the event's occurring by choosing to walk somewhere that was ideal for an ambush.

Some of the delegates on my workshops go to great lengths to proclaim their complete innocence of any potential contribution to the issues pertaining to their vital conversation. In 90% of cases, when I ask them to think systemically at the very least they realise that their procrastination over having the vital conversation and letting the issue fester is a passive yet highly valid input on their part.

When you are courageous enough to put your hand up and share with the other person your input to a problem, you are demonstrating that your focus has shifted from blaming them to mutual understanding and ownership. This in turn opens the door to a safer space, increasing the likelihood of the other person acknowledging their own inputs to the issue.

A safer approach to understanding everyone's inputs

But what if you own up to your contribution and the other person simply agrees, saying that you're absolutely right, it is all your fault? If that happens to you more than once, you may well quickly fall back into the relative safety of blaming the other person.

The key to retaining the focus on how you have both contributed is in how you phrase this aspect of your vital conversation. Rather than simply sharing your inputs, I recommend saying something similar to below, changing the wording to suit your situation.

"Claire, as I see it we have both contributed to your project deadline not being met. I also believe that there are two external factors that have affected the timelines."

If I know that Claire is someone who has previously demonstrated a high level of integrity and personal accountability, I would show faith and create a safer space by sharing my input to the issue first. However, if I have reservations over Claire's willingness to take ownership, then I would word the next part similarly to this:

"Claire, as I see it we have both contributed to your project deadline not being met. I also believe that there are two external factors that have affected the timelines. First I'd like to share with you how I believe you have contributed to our current position, and then I'd like to hear from you if you see that differently. I'm also keen to share how I have contributed and to hear if you think I've missed anything."

The way you approach this will be highly dependent on your particular situation. If there is relationship baggage or the other person has been badly burned by a corporate blame culture, then they are likely still to be defensive and to go into blame.

A shift in mindset, not a technique

If you see systems or input thinking as a great technique to get people to own up to their mistakes, then in reality you're just treating it as a rebranded version of blame and the other person will quickly realise that blame and punishment are still at the heart of your intention. When you are truly thinking systemically, you operate on the basis of deep curiosity powered by the underlying assumption that you cannot truly know what the other person is thinking or has experienced or the situational factors that may have influenced their actions, therefore you cannot be 100% sure of all the inputs to this particular situation. Because you also know that in the vast majority of cases you have contributed to the issues involved, you have the opportunity to share those inputs so that the other person can draw their conclusions from a richer and more relevant view of the whole.

This shift in mindset and the accompanying skills are unlikely to feel comfortable when you try them for the first couple of times. You may initially struggle to find the right words and end up either not realising a shared vision of inputs or having a conversation that still has moments in which blame swings back into play. But the rewards of a systemic approach are worth the effort, and it will begin to build trust as the other party witnesses at first hand your desire to move away from blame and towards a deeper understanding of the issues.

 Back to your VC coaching tool: Answer section 11

Step 6: Do you know what you want?

You may think what you want from your vital conversation is obvious, but in reality it can be somewhat of a minefield. Clarifying what you want is partly a process of deduction, partly having the right mindset. You'd be amazed how many people go into high-stakes conversations determined to tell the other person what's wrong, who's to blame and what they don't want to happen in the future.

It's hard to stress just how important this step is. Not only will it set the tone of your vital conversation, it will shape the way you prepare for the conversation as a whole. It's also essential to mention that it isn't enough simply to know what outcome you want for the conversation and then doggedly stick to it. As you're about to see, being purely outcome driven can generate unnecessary conflict and damage your relationship.

Context is key

How fixed your outcome is depends on the situation. For instance, there's a world of difference between a vital conversation where you're firing someone and a discussion with your 15-year-old daughter about the level of intimacy she wishes to experience in the family home with her new 18-year-old boyfriend.

So you first have to decide what type of conversation you need to have. If it's any of the following examples, your outcome is likely to be specific and fixed:

❖ Making someone redundant.
❖ Giving specific, verifiable feedback to an underperforming employee.
❖ Passing on bad news (e.g. the death of a loved one).
❖ Ending a relationship (that you are 100% sure you want to end).
❖ Closing down a contract with a supplier.

Just because the outcome is non-negotiable doesn't necessarily mean that the way in which you decide to have the conversation can't still come from a third-generation approach. Even when you're telling someone they're losing their job, compassion for their feelings and curiosity about how they have received your news will increase the chances of a more productive conversation and minimise any damage to the ongoing relationship. (More on this can be found in Chapter 14: Giving Bad News.)

Top tip: Double check a non-negotiable

When the stakes are significant and emotions are running high, it is quite possible to convince yourself that you have to deliver a non-negotiable outcome. Perhaps you want to end a relationship but are scared to encourage an open, two-way dialogue, as it might throw up some home truths you'd rather not face. If you sense that you've had a very strong, knee-jerk reaction to an issue and have become stuck in a non-negotiable stance, ask yourself: "What am I afraid of that might be driving this command-and-control approach?"

The corporate mantra: Solutions, solutions, solutions!

In my days as an employee of a big corporate, if I had a pound for every time a manager or trainer told me or the team to be "solutions oriented", I'd be a millionaire by now. Rather than focusing on the problem, they said, you need to become a pro-active, solutions-based thinker.

You may think this is common sense, and as I've already said the search for solutions has obvious benefits, but it also led to unnecessary conflict as well-intentioned managers slaved over PowerPoint presentations for hours and became increasingly attached to their fantastic propositions. When those solutions were challenged by someone else (who was rather attached to their own solution), significant differences of opinion and arguments were the result. As the emotion and attachment increased, what started out as a well-intentioned way forward became a non-negotiable stance even though it did not need to be. At this point either the person with the higher authority pulled rank, or in many cases a compromise was agreed that didn't meet either party's or the organisation's true needs.

The same effect can occur in your vital conversations. You may have invested a lot of effort in formulating what you see as a genuine win/win solution. But you need to realise that what might seem a fair and solid option to you may not be accepted as a viable option by the other person.

What are involved here are positions versus interests. A position is a single answer or solution to a problem, whereas interests are the needs, concerns or hopes that people have invested in a given situation. Positions tend to hide individual interests.

Case study: Positions versus interests

Samrah and Jalil are discussing where to spend a summer weekend break.

SAMRAH: Let's fly down to the south of France to a 5-star, fully inclusive beach resort.

JALIL: You know I hate those stuff-your-face buffet places, I get so bored. Why don't we go to Ireland and do some walking and biking?

SAMRAH: What is it with you, always having to be on the go? Can't you take a few days off and chill out?

JALIL: Exercise is how I relax. The last time we went on one of your lie-on-the-beach holidays I came back like a coiled-up spring. It didn't feel like a holiday at all.

SAMRAH: That's my point, you just don't know how to relax.

The challenge when focusing on solutions is that the positions can often be in conflict even though the underlying interests are not. Jalil and Samrah are locked in a conversational logjam where each is defending their own position. Very quickly both parties begin to dig in, and become frustrated as each begins to believe that the other isn't listening or doesn't care about what's important to them. Sadly, the eventual outcome may be that one grinds the other into conceding. Alternatively, one party may value a harmonious relationship more than getting the holiday they want, so they give in but end up feeling resentful. Finally, a common occurrence is that that the argument leads them to pick a holiday destination that's actually an unnecessary and unsatisfactory compromise that doesn't meet either person's needs.

The missing piece of the puzzle: Your needs

Rather than going from identifying the problem to defining a solution or position immediately, you need to take a further step that is crucial but easy to overlook. The missing element creates a three-stage thinking process:

1. Define the issue or problem.
2. Work out the underlying needs, concerns and interests that you want met.
3. Think through potential ideas and options to meet your needs, but avoid "my way or the highway", rigid solutions.

You may have to dig deep to find your needs. Take another look at the iceberg model opposite. You can see that below your feelings are your needs and your interests. Provided that you don't allow your unchallenged mental stories to overtake you by the way

they often have a rigid, "the issue must be solved this way" attitude embedded within them, you can begin to get in touch with your real needs and interests using the following approach.

First, become very clear about the issue in factual terms, removing any emotive story that may be clouding your thoughts.

Then use two questions to connect with your interests:

1. What is most important to me about the issues?
2. Can I list what the most important criteria are that a potential solution must meet?

If you're doing this for the first time it may take a while for the interests to crystallise as words in your minds. This is natural and your powers of deduction will sharpen over time. You might find it useful to return to the list of needs on page 85, as many of the solutions you craft are unconsciously designed to meet your core psychological needs (e.g. security, understanding, purpose, respect).

Be careful to get down to pinpointing the deeper need rather than something that would help you to meet that need. For example, if you're thinking "My need is for money", ask yourself, "What would money give or do for me?" You might then deduce that money will give you security or recognition; which would be the deeper psychological need? It may be that money is still a key factor in the conversation, but you may also realise that there are other solutions or alternatives to money that might still give you security or recognition.

Top tip

If you're really stuck in solution mode, think through your solution and ask this question:

3. If the other person agrees to my solution, what does that give me, do for me or mean to me?

This is a way of reversing out from the solution into your interests.

A great bonus comes from generating an interests-based dialogue. As you will see in the next chapter, rather than forcing your solution you will be asking questions to understand what is most important to the other person. You will also share your interests, giving the other person an opportunity to have a wider base of information and a further understanding of what's really important to you. This approach builds trust and a kind of creative spaciousness, opening up the floor to collaborative thinking and higher levels of commitment to a joint solution.

Interests, intentions and purpose

So at this stage of your preparation you have become clearer about your underlying interests. This is a good time to compare these interests with your previous work on intentions and pull that together to clarify your overall purpose for this conversation.

As your coach and mentor, I now want to ask you the following questions:

1. Is there a happy marriage between your interests and your stated intentions?
2. Based on your interests and intentions, what is your overriding purpose in having this vital conversation?

Back to your VC coaching tool: Answer sections 12–15

Step 7: Getting off on the right foot

"On this path it's only the first step that counts."
St Jean-Baptiste-Marie Vianney

Talk to any gymnast, figure skater or 100-metre runner about how they build the foundations of a great performance and they will emphasise just how much time and energy they invest in making sure that they make the best possible start.

The beginning of a vital conversation can be emotionally demanding for both parties. You can never be sure how the other person will react, or what they may say or want from you. The conversation may involve giving or receiving candid feedback. There may be baggage from previous negative encounters with this person or a painful conversation of this kind that didn't go well in the past.

The nature of the opening will depend on the context you find yourself in. Here are some possible situations:

❖ You have asked the other person to have this conversation with you.
❖ They have asked you to have this conversation with them.
❖ They have sprung the conversation on you with no notice.
❖ You have sprung the conversation on them with no notice.

I recommend that you avoid dropping an impromptu vital conversation on someone else unless it meets one of the following three criteria:

1. The consequences of not having the conversation immediately are very severe.
2. The content of or reason for having the conversation has a high possibility of creating so much anxiety in the other person that they may become too stressed out if they have to wait several hours or days to have the conversation.
3. You know with certainty that the moment you mention wanting to have the conversation, the other person will insist on having it there and then.

As this book is written from the stance that it is you who wishes to initiate a vital conversation, let us look at the scenario where your intention is to give the other person notice of a future conversation.

The conversation before the conversation

If you're choosing to give the other person prior notice, this task is in itself a conversation. I recommend keeping this as brief as possible while still giving enough information to avoid being perceived as elusive.

Here is my suggestion, but it is important to bear in mind that you must find your own words and sequencing rather than rigidly following mine, as only you know the issues and context you find yourself in.

In a succinct way:

1. Let the other person know that you want to talk about something that's very important to you.
2. In two sentences or fewer, name the issue you want to talk about. Keep your story and judgements or solutions to yourself and simply remain as close to the facts as possible.

3. Share your reasoning behind wanting to have this conversation.

4. Let them know that you don't want to have the conversation now but wish to give them some time to think about the issue before talking it through.

5. Attempt to confirm that they have heard you correctly by asking them to share their understanding of what you've asked for. (It's important to remember that what you said may not be what they heard.)

6. Confirm that they're OK with what you've asked for and arrange a mutually convenient time to have the conversation.

However, be fully prepared for the conversation just in case. Even if the other person is completely OK with having the conversation later, they may have questions they want to ask that will help them in their preparations. It's also possible that you get an unexpectedly adverse reaction. Your preparation will help you either stay strong and refuse to be drawn into a full-blown conversation or, if appropriate, discuss certain elements of the issue with them there and then.

How not to kick off your conversation

When you do begin the vital conversation itself, you need to be fully prepared. If you haven't done your preparation or you're not in control of your emotional state, you run the risk of derailing the whole conversation in two possible ways:

❖ Going round the houses. You ease into the conversation very slowly and take an age to get round to the real issues you want to talk about. All the while the other person, in the absence of concrete facts or direction, is racing up their own ladder of inference and making all kinds of assumptions.

❖ Justifying the conversation from inside your biased story. When you start the conversation from your own story, you run the risk of downloading your untested assumptions, moralistic judgements and blame onto the other person. This is likely to trigger a defensive reaction, where they feel the need to justify their own story and the conversation inevitably sinks into argumentative quicksand.

Your vital conversation: 90 seconds or less

You have around 90 seconds or ideally less to explain your reason for needing the conversation. There are four good reasons for this:

❖ If you take more than 90 seconds, the other person is likely to start going up their own mental ladder and make unresourceful assumptions about this high-stakes conversation.
❖ It's hard for the other person to listen for more than 90 seconds as their ability to take on board what you're saying diminishes rapidly beyond that time.
❖ The time guideline encourages you to become very specific and generates more transparency, as there is no time for padding out.
❖ After 90 seconds the other person may become restless or anxious and start butting in, which will not make you feel heard.

You need to find the right words for your situation, but I recommend including the following:

❖ Define the issue and your purpose for having the conversation.
❖ Express what you believe to be at stake and any consequences.
❖ Include how you feel about this issue and potentially the conversation.
❖ Express your motivation to find a positive way forward.
❖ Create the beginnings of a collaborative role for the other person by inviting them to respond to what you have just said.
❖ Even if you have a non-negotiable outcome, attempt to decide together how you will have the conversation.

Case study: Getting to the point

Here's an example of the start of a conversation between Fran, a sales manager, and Hannah, one of her junior sales consultants.

"Hannah, I want to discuss with you today your sales performance over the last two quarters. The figures show that your sales results are dropping each month and if you can't turn this around then I believe your job is at stake. I'm kind of frustrated because my gut instincts tell me that you have got what it takes to make these targets, but I'm also confused about why your results are lower than I would have hoped for. I would really like to find a positive way forward today. But before we get into the detail, I'd like to get your take on what I've just said. Do let me know if you see anything that I've said differently."

This took around 53 seconds. Fran got to the point, so she didn't leave Hannah guessing about the nature or importance of the conversation. She opened up to how she was feeling and backed that up with her true intention to find a way forward. Finally, she began to encourage a more collaborative approach to discussing the performance issues, respecting that Hannah would have her own take on things. She even encouraged Hannah to challenge her perception of the situation.

You may also have noticed that Fran minimises her use of judgemental statements such as "not good enough", "poor" or "ineffective" and instead uses neutral language about Hannah's results. Fran realises that these emotive words are only likely to inflame Hannah's internal mental stories, creating fear or defensiveness. She has learned the art of describing the issues and conversation in the way a third-party mediator would. A skilled mediator realises that emotions will be running high at the beginning of a dispute and therefore is ultra careful to eliminate judgements or biases that may act as a trigger to either party.

Give the other person space

Even if you have done a great job of positioning the conversation, you can never be quite sure how the other person will respond. Think back to a time where someone engaged you in a difficult conversation. Can you remember what it was like to absorb what they were saying and how your brain worked overtime not only to make sense of the messages but also to attempt to formulate a response? When you put yourself in someone else's shoes you can have more empathy for the feeling of being overwhelmed that they can experience during a conversation of this nature.

In the case study above, Fran gives Hannah time to reflect and some air time to verbalise her feelings. Don't be surprised if what initially comes back from the other person is jumbled or tainted with strong emotion, as they may still be processing what you have said.

Creating space for the other person also sends the message that you respect what they have to say. Even when it looks like they have finished responding, let there be a few seconds of silence. Those extra moments either allow them to talk a little more or at the very least show that you are not in a rush to take charge or dominate the conversation.

Practise, practice, practise!

When I am asked to mentor a CEO on a vital conversation, I ask them to practise their start with me and record it. It's amazing how many times even a highly experienced director needs to practise before they can deliver an effective, concise start. Fortunately, when they hear their early attempts and compare them with the much improved later version, they understand why I say practise, practise, practise!

Some workshop delegates are worried that practising will make them robotic. My experience shows that actually you become more fluent and sound more human – provided that you are still coming to your conversation with the intention to make it work for both parties. If you don't practise, then it's likely that your nerves will take over and you will either talk from your biased, judgemental story or go round and round the houses without naming the real issues you need to discuss.

Top tip

Beg, borrow or steal a digital voice recorder, write out your start pretty much word for word and then record yourself. When you replay your start it will provide invaluable feedback that will enable you to hone and improve that initial opening. I had one CEO re-record his start 16 times, but he later commented that his final version made a huge difference to the overall success of his actual vital conversation.

Back to your VC coaching tool: Answer section 16

10
Understanding the Dynamics

"Understanding is a happy accident, misunderstanding is the norm."   *Anonymous*

Now that you've done your preparation, this chapter will enhance that by highlighting the mindset, behaviours and skills that will significantly boost the odds of your navigating your vital conversation to a successful conclusion. More specifically, this chapter will:

❖ Unpack the dynamics of what will mentally and physically occur between you and the other person.
❖ Encourage you to start your vital conversation from a third-generation mindset.

Snakes and ladders

Vital conversations are rarely linear. They're much more akin to the children's board game snakes and ladders. Issues can be complex and you can never be 100% sure how you or the other person will react to new information, conflicting opinions or a spike of unanticipated emotion. In the blink of an eye you land on a verbal snake and the conversation can plummet into free fall. Alternatively, there will also be times when your dialogue creates a moment of joint understanding or resolves an impasse and together you accelerate up a ladder, nearer to a successful outcome.

Since it's highly unlikely that your vital conversation will go from A to B without a hitch, you need an alternative to the second-generation approach that prescribes a sausage machine of using certain covert skills in a certain order in order to gain a certain outcome. I advocate the use of a highly flexible "Swiss army knife" of skills that you can apply wherever you find yourself in the conversation. The first skill is to understand the background to what is going to happen in the conversation itself.

Conversational dynamics

It helps to understand what is going on inside both parties' heads during high-stakes conversations. Let me explain with the aid of the diagram overleaf.

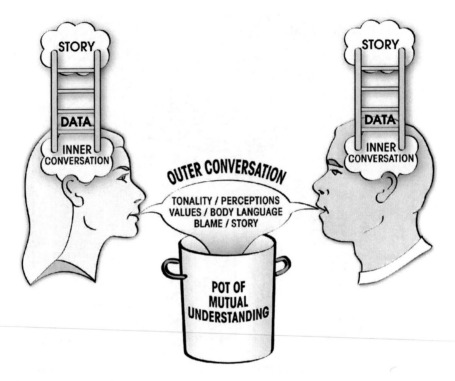

Three conversations not one

Although you have the physical exchange of words, each party will also be having a private conversation with themselves in the recesses of their own mind. So in reality there are not one but three conversations taking place. This inner dialogue is what you are both thinking and feeling, but not necessarily sharing with each other. The long-term goal as your confidence and skill grow will be to achieve two things:

❖ To get as much of your inner thoughts and feelings as you can into the conversation in a safe and respectful way.
❖ To explore and clarify the inner thoughts, assumptions and feelings of the other person, also in a safe and respectful way.

Getting all the relevant information into the conversation creates more understanding, empathy and trust for each person's situation, which become the building blocks of joint problem solving.

Two ladders

I have already covered how easy it is for you to create stories or attribute motives or judgements to the other person. In a vital conversation, you have the added complication of two human beings who are both capable of simultaneously racing up their own private ladders of inference, creating hidden and untested assumptions about the issues at hand or the other person's behaviour.

Multifaceted dialogue

You will see from the diagram that the communication flowing in the "outer conversation" is more than just words. If you were to place it under a metaphorical microscope you would see the building blocks of a challenging conversation, including tonality, judgements, perceptions, blame, feelings, solutions and personal values, to name but a few. Once again, being able to objectively identify these components will enable you to gain perspective on whatever is thrown at you. When someone says "This is all your fault!" it makes all the difference to keeping your cool if your higher self, or the observer within as I call it, can say "OK, I can see that they are choosing to blame me", rather than being hijacked by an automatic inner reaction that might go "How dare they blame me? What about when they did/didn't, should/shouldn't have…"

Mutual understanding is the goal

When you use a third-generation mindset to guide your use of the skills presented in this book, your goal is to create a reservoir of shared understanding between you and the other person. This does not mean you will necessarily see eye to eye on all the issues, but exploring their story and sharing your own will produce common ground from which new understandings, ideas and mutually beneficial ways forward can be crafted.

When two worlds collide

How do you develop curiosity for the other person's perception of reality?

Take a look at the picture above. If you relax your gaze long enough, you may begin to make out the hidden image.

Take a look at the sign below. What does it say?

So what did you see in the first picture: a man with a hat, a dog's face, a horse, nothing at all? The central image is actually a cowboy riding a horse (see the image revealed on page 244).

In the second image, did you read "I love Paris in the spring time"? If you did, have another look at the number of "the"s.

In today's world you are bombarded with so much information that in order to function effectively, you have to become highly selective about what you pay attention to. Each person has their own way of filtering their day-to-day experiences.

Just like with the images, the parties in a vital conversation may have conflicting perspectives on the issues involved. There are times in high-stakes conversations when you know deep down that you are in the right. But here's the dilemma: the other person is usually feeling exactly the same!

The right–wrong paradigm

There are many occasions on which people don't agree with your point of view, and often you don't really care. You may also like to see yourself as someone who encourages others' opinions and feel that it's healthy to have your own views challenged. That's fine when the stakes are low, but when the other person's differing opinions have a potentially negative impact on your life, career or business, you might not be eager to be so democratic. The moment you begin to feel that you are going to lose something that is psychologically or materially important to you, it is incredibly easy to shift from "I wonder how they see this" to "They are wrong" or in some cases "Are they blind/mad/stupid/crazy?"

Real-life case study: Afraid of being wrong

A workshop delegate recently had a "light bulb moment" about his right–wrong thinking. The exercise was to debate the UK's involvement in the Iraq war. The delegates held opposing views but had to listen to how the other person saw the situation, carefully summarising what they had heard before they could give their opinion.

In the debriefing, this delegate said that he had found the exercise very challenging. When I asked him to elaborate, he explained that he'd prepared some very persuasive points of view but had also committed to listen carefully to the other person's reasoning.

"So what was the problem?" I asked.

He replied, "It was a nightmare. As I took in what they were saying, I suddenly realised they had a brilliant point of view."

As the workshop facilitator I responded, "So how was that challenging for you?"

He answered, "But doesn't that make me wrong."

At that instant he realised that his addiction to needing to be right was less about his belief in his own point of view and more to do with the fear of being exposed as wrong!

In the group discussion that followed, other delegates shared their fears of being seen as wrong, weak or vulnerable. It dawned on the group that when you put your ego to one side and become fully open to someone else's point of view, you can move beyond your conditioned fears and realise that a different view is not necessarily a threat but an opportunity to experience a broader, richer and more diverse world.

I can empathise completely with the importance of making good decisions. Nevertheless, if you remain open to how others see things, you collate more relevant information and create a more complete picture from which better-informed decisions can be made.

When you are stuck in the "I'm right, you're wrong" paradigm, your conversation can quickly degenerate into arguments and defensive positions. The choices available to you when you operate from this mode all have negative side effects. If you have more authority you can use power to enforce a decision, but that's likely to diminish the long-term relationship. You can back down and accommodate the other person's wishes, but that usually leaves you feeling resentful. You can reach some form of compromise that may appear fair, yet it rarely feels particularly satisfactory for either party.

The answer is to realise that the success of a vital conversation is not about identifying who's right or wrong. You could argue until the cows came home and on many occasions you wouldn't even be able to agree on what the facts really mean. Making progress is more about understanding perceptions and acknowledging feelings, hopes and fears.

To do this you need to shift into a third-generation mindset and access the curiosity that enables your inner dialogue to ask "How are they seeing this differently?" or "What am I missing or not understanding here?" Yet to attain this new state of mind, you must first let go of your old paradigms – and that means releasing your need to be right.

Here are three considerations to help you make the shift.

People interpret the same information differently

When I say the word "dog" to you, what image comes into your mind? Perhaps it's a cuddly puppy, your own pet. For some it may be something smelly, dirty or even with a large set of snarling teeth. The same input generates different reactions.

In Tony Robbins' book *Awaken the Giant Within*, he recalls being present at a rare solar eclipse. He made the interesting observation that moments after the eclipse had occurred, some people watching were overwhelmed by the beauty and magic of the event, whereas others were complaining that it had not been as perfect as the astronomers had predicted. The eclipse was basically the same physical event for everyone, but their individual interpretations were worlds apart.

A couple are having marriage counselling and they are arguing about the levels of sexual intimacy in their relationship.
The woman says, "We hardly ever have sex any more."
The man responds, "That's rubbish, we have it all the time."
At this point the therapist asks, "So how often do you have sex?"
Both partners simultaneously reply, "Once a week."

Even hard facts and data can and will be interpreted differently by you and the other person.

People operate from different rules

In many personal, working and business partnerships, the people involved are unaware of the unconscious rules that are influencing their own and the other person's behaviour. You have your own rules about all kinds of things (time keeping, tidiness, cleanliness, meetings, finances, raising kids, manners, driving styles and so on). People even have rules about how they like to be appreciated, recognised and loved.

Real-life case study: Unspoken rules

Brian and Pete are four months into their relationship. They have enjoyed a long and happy "honeymoon" period where neither could do any wrong. They are well matched, with shared values and interests, but Pete is becoming increasingly frustrated and even a little embarrassed about Brian's behaviour in front of friends when he's had a few too many to drink.

Fortunately, both Pete and Brian value honest and transparent communication. They unconsciously adopted this value from watching their parents. However, in Pete's family the unspoken rule for engaging in such a discussion would be that you always conveyed your concerns in a calm fashion, keeping emotion to a minimum. What you never did was raise your voice or lose control. In fact, in Pete's family if things became heated people agreed to walk away and cool off for a while. Brian's family also lived out the value of honest, transparent communication, but the unconscious rules of engagement were that you wore your heart on your sleeve and told people exactly how it was for you. In Brian's family if you expressed emotion and became increasingly vocal, it simply showed how much you cared. What you never did was negate the other person's feelings or, even worse, walk away if the matter was not yet resolved.

You can guess the rest of this story. Pete calmly raises the issue. Brian, working from his family conditioning, comes back strong and loud with his point of view. Pete asks Brian to calm down and Brian begins to develop an inner story about how Pete is negating his feelings, so he tells him in a loud and emotional voice not to be so insensitive. Pete walks away and Brian explodes!

Here we have two people who share the same value but have very different rules for how that value is met.

I'm not saying you should spend the next ten years of your life in therapy working out all your rules. What I am saying is that your undisclosed or unconscious rules play a significant role in the way you interpret or judge both the issues and the other person's behaviour.

Before you begin a vital conversation, it's worth asking yourself the following questions:

* ❖ What hidden rules or expectations of mine are at play in this situation?
* ❖ What effect are they having on my appreciation of the issues or the other person in this conversation?
* ❖ Would the other person be aware of the rules or expectations I am operating from?
* ❖ Are the rules fair/reasonable or are they historical baggage that is past its sell-by date and should be challenged?
* ❖ Could the other party have hidden rules or expectations that are different from mine?

People have access to different information

It's obvious that you can never know the other person better than they know themselves. You were not party to how they were raised, and even their sister or brother will not fully understand how they interpret their life experiences. In the same way, they cannot possibly understand you as well as you know yourself. They do not know all your fears, vulnerabilities, hopes and dreams. They do not have complete, uncensored access to your current life challenges, work pressures or home life issues.

Remember John and Michael, the business partners in the advertising agency (page 88)? John is unaware that Michael has been up all night with his 1 year old and that his wife has been unwell so he has had to shoulder not just his day job but also many family commitments. In turn, Michael is unaware that John has cancelled a dinner date with his wife and worked late into the night to get the figures ready for the meeting and that he has diary commitments that leave no room for overruns.

When you come from a deep wellspring of curiosity, you stay open to the fact that the other person's behaviour or decisions may be partially or wholly driven by external situational factors. You therefore don't fall into the trap of attributing their faults to personality flaws. So John would ask "I wonder what factors could have prevented Michael from being here on time?" rather than complaining "He is lazy and not a team player!".

Willpower is not enough

If you have ever tried to kick off a new exercise and diet programme that was driven by willpower alone, you may well have experienced how increasingly challenging it became to keep picking up that gym bag and munching through those salads. Unless the new health regime is supported by a deep-seated shift in your mindset in the way you view exercise and nourish your body, most people under the daily pressures of life revert to old eating habits and a predominantly sedentary lifestyle.

It's similar with the transformation required to become more effective in high-stakes conversations. Attempting to reach a genuine understanding of where the other person is coming from may require you not just to increase your listening but to be able to hear messages that you strongly disagree with or could make you feel insecure. Using willpower to remain curious and open is an admirable endeavour, but when the pressure's really on most people go back to habitual modes of first- and second-generation thinking.

Install the upgrade

To get a significant, sustainable improvement in the effectiveness of your vital conversations, you need to upgrade your mental software. If you go back to the iceberg model, you know that the story you tell yourself drives your needs, feelings, behaviours and the results you achieve. So change the fundamental story or the underlying assumptions from which you operate and in turn you change the way you behave in a vital conversation.

Curiosity

If you think about it, it verges on arrogance to believe that your version of events (your story) is the correct one. My evidence for this bold statement is that it's simply not possible for any one person to be in sole possession of all the facts and circumstances. At the very least, you certainly cannot have a flawless take on how the other person will be perceiving the issues and facts, or the situational pressures they may be under.

More than 60 years ago, F. Scott Fitzgerald said that the "ability to hold two opposing ideas in mind at the same time and still retain the ability to function" was the sign of a truly intelligent individual. Whether or not you agree with his point of view, the ability to think integratively – the ability to hold two points of view with the possibility of combining them to create a more complete "third view" – is a major mental shift in how you approach the conversation. In my view, to achieve this it's imperative to operate from a foundation of heightened curiosity. To generate this innate curious behaviour, the following underlying assumptions are useful:

- ❖ I bring certain information and assumptions to the conversation, others will bring different information and assumptions.
- ❖ We may both perceive even the same information in different ways.
- ❖ Staying open to new and relevant information increases both parties' understanding.
- ❖ If we recognise our differences, we can learn and grow.

From these assumptions, it is obvious that no one person can have a monopoly on right or wrong. Instead, your mindset shifts from "I am right" to "How are we are seeing this differently?". This is what Roger Schwarz terms "sharing all relevant information". The goal becomes a balance between making sure that you understand what's going on for the other person (understanding their story) while at the same time finding ways to get your own non-judgemental story, needs and feelings into the conversation.

Compassion

There will be times when the other party's behaviour makes it difficult for you to remain curious and open. They may be deeply rooted in a command-and-control, second-generation mindset or behave in ways that really offend your own rules about respectful interaction. It's at times like these when you need to operate from the following core assumptions:

❖ The other party is communicating at their best. If they knew better they would do better.

❖ When the other person's behaviour is difficult to deal with, I have compassion for what I feel and need.

Some of my workshop delegates comment that they work with people who do know better and behave in destructive ways on purpose. I would not disagree that a very small percentage of people are malicious in their communication. Yet even these people are currently operating from their best, because if they actually had a higher level of consciousness about the worth of and respect for their fellow human beings, they wouldn't act in the ways they do. I also believe that under enough pressure everyone can communicate in ways that are damaging or destructive. As Marshall Rosenberg suggests, it's at these moments that you need to have the compassion to see the human being that lies behind the behaviour. Remember to "see them beautiful".

At the same time, you have to develop compassion for yourself. With the self-awareness and emotional state management tools that I outline in Chapters 5–8, if the other person does not reciprocate the air time you are willing to give them, you can recognise your frustration. If you are compassionate towards yourself, you can acknowledge the emotion, stay present and remain committed to finding a productive way forward.

Top tip: "Fascinating"

I have been in many conversations when the other party's behaviour has been extremely challenging to be in the presence of, let alone handle. At times like these I use a strategy that reduces the chances of a counterproductive reaction on my part. When I encounter behaviour that I perceive as challenging, I secretly say "Fascinating!" or "Fascinating behaviour" to myself. I use a slightly sarcastic internal dialogue tone that helps me smile on the inside at what I am observing. I don't do this to mock the other person, it simply acts as a psychological intermission or breathing space between their behaviour and a potential knee-jerk reaction from me. If you combine "Fascinating" with three or four diaphragmatic breaths, you may be surprised just how well you begin to handle such moments.

Courage

Increasing your capability to engage in vital conversations is not just a one-way street of becoming a better listener. If you are going to share all the relevant information on the basis of which both sides can understand the situation more clearly, you also have to have courage. There will be opportunities in the conversation when it is crucial to convey what is most important to you. This is not just beneficial for your own sanity, it also allows the other person to gain a more comprehensive view of your needs and motivations.

Once again, there are some underlying mental software or assumptions that I recommend you install:

❖ I have the right to respectfully communicate my needs, feelings and point of view.
❖ I encourage others to respectfully enquire into, clarify and challenge my own point of view.

❖ I have the right to respectfully enquire into, clarify and challenge the other person's point of view.

Connect with the other person's core psychological needs

The nature of high-stakes conversations, differing opinions and
uncertainty inevitably generates powerful emotions and even fear
in the other person, even before the first word is spoken. In this
unresourceful state they may be stressed, defensive or at the very
least distracted, making productive two-way dialogue all the more
unlikely. So how do you create a resourceful, respectful and safe
space that increases the likelihood of a successful conversation?

About six years ago I came across a diagram called the journey of influence, and I've found it to be an invaluable way of
explaining the importance of both you and the other person being
in a resourceful state of mind.

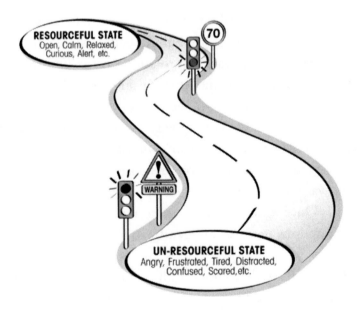

Reproduced with permission from RogenSi

Imagine this scenario. You are about to enter your colleague's office and engage in a vital conversation. You have had enough self-awareness to acknowledge your own feelings and have used some of the state management strategies in this book to get your mind and body in a resourceful space. However, before you open the door, can you be 100% sure you know what mood the other person is likely to be in? If they know the nature of the imminent conversation, they may be feeling anxious or defensive. Even if they are completely unaware of the importance of the conversation you are about to initiate, they may well be in an unresourceful state from a previous meeting or another life event that has influenced their mood. It's crucial at this point that you tune into and become sensitive to the other person's emotional state.

Have you ever tried to engage in constructive dialogue with someone when they are angry, anxious, tired or defensive? My experience is that when someone is in an unresourceful place, the chances of productive dialogue are a little less than zero. You will notice near the bottom of the model that the traffic light is on red and there's a warning triangle! Too often in my role as a mediator I see parties in conflict who show little or no awareness of each other's emotional state. Instead of being empathic to the other person's feelings by listening and understanding, they become increasingly agitated and push their viewpoint even harder, thus creating a mutual downward spiral of frustration that merely serves to exaggerate their negative disposition.

In Chapter 6 I discussed how feelings are partly driven by the degree to which you are able to meet your core psychological needs. Listed below are some classic examples:

Understanding	Respect
Recognition	Consideration
Fairness	Safety
Security	Freedom
Meaning/purpose	Fun

Learning   Belonging
Clarity   Autonomy

Recall a time when you were in a conversation in which the issues were important to you but you didn't feel like the other person was listening. As you remember that conversation, take a look at the list of needs above and ask yourself which were not being met by the other person's poor listening. Common ones expressed in this context are respect, understanding, recognition and fairness. If your need for respect or understanding was not met, for example, it probably created feelings of frustration or at the very least disappointment.

Now think back to when someone took the time to listen carefully to what you had to say. Would it be fair to say that your need for understanding, consideration or respect was met by their attentiveness? Think back to how you felt when you had those needs met: calm, relaxed, content? In this emotional space, are you more or less likely to be open to what another person has to say?

Going back to the journey of influence diagram, feelings of being open, curious and calm are what I would describe as both parties entering a resourceful state. At the top of the model the traffic light has turned to green, as it's likely that effective dialogue and hence more progress can now take place. Just because both parties are now in a more receptive and open space there is no guarantee that you will reach a positive outcome, but it does give you a fighting chance of creating a conversational climate that fosters a greater possibility of success.

So the journey of influence diagram highlights that if you are willing to listen to the other person's story, you will begin to meet some of their core psychological needs (respect, understanding, fairness etc.). By you meeting these needs the other person will experience a shift in emotions, feeling calmer and more relaxed. They will begin to feel more reassured that you care about their point of view and potentially they start to become more open to what you have to say. Of course, they won't have read this book, so they may initially not do such a good job of listening to you. But with a little patience and a genuine desire to listen, you can create an atmosphere that is more conducive to both parties being heard.

Integrity moment!

Connecting with another person's core emotional needs is incredibly powerful and at this juncture you face a choice. A second-generation mindset sees this as a chance to manipulate the other person into a more receptive state so that you can meet your own objectives, in essence lining them up for the kill. From a third-generation mindset your intention is to meet both parties' core needs, creating an emotionally resourceful space for mutual understanding and collaborative problem solving.

Keep asking yourself this question: "Am I connecting to the other person's core needs for the benefit of both of us?"

Part IV

The Conversation

11

The Stages of a Vital Conversation

Although vital conversations rarely go from A to B in a straight line, it can be helpful to map out some distinct stages that you have to pass through if you are to increase your chances of a positive outcome. This chapter gives a brief description of each stage.

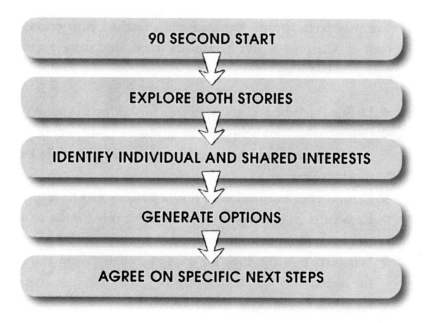

- 90 SECOND START
- EXPLORE BOTH STORIES
- IDENTIFY INDIVIDUAL AND SHARED INTERESTS
- GENERATE OPTIONS
- AGREE ON SPECIFIC NEXT STEPS

You don't need to work through these stages mechanically, but be aware that if you skip a stage or cut it short, there may be consequences. For instance, if you don't attempt to understand and share both parties' stories, you may not have enough joint understanding and trust to brainstorm viable options for moving forward.

Also be aware that the other person will not be consciously following this roadmap. In my experience they are likely to want a lot of air time to talk about how they see things (their story), possibly throw in some explicit or implicit blame and repeatedly put forward their suggestions, solutions and advice (most of which probably won't work for you!). If this happens, try to stay connected to the values of compassion and curiosity from the third-generation approach and remind yourself that they may not have had the benefit of reading this book.

The 90-second start

You may have already prepared and practised your concise start back in Chapter 9, but as a quick reminder, these are the key points to include:

❖ Define the issue and your purpose for having the conversation.
❖ Express what you believe to be at stake and any consequences.
❖ If appropriate and safe, reveal how you feel about the issues or the conversation.
❖ Express your motivation to find a positive way forward.
❖ Create the beginnings of a collaborative role for the other person by inviting them to respond.
❖ Wherever possible, look for ways to co-design how you discuss the issues.
❖ Keep your opening to under 90 seconds.

Top tip: Handling a strong outburst

If the other person has a strong emotional or defensive reaction, remember the following:

❖ Breathe into your diaphragm and see the human being behind the behaviour.

❖ Make a tentative guess at how they might be feeling: "You seem very frustrated that the decision was made without your involvement."
❖ Ask them to expand on their concerns (give them some air time): "Can you tell me more about how you are seeing this differently?"
❖ Connect to their core needs by paraphrasing what they've said to demonstrate that you genuinely care about their concerns or frustrations.
❖ Restate your needs and hopes for the conversation.

There's more on dealing with outbursts in Chapter 12.

Explore both stories

"Listen or thy tongue will keep the deaf."
American Indian proverb

This stage is about discovering and sharing all relevant information and increasing the reservoir of mutual understanding. The more relevant information you can provide, the better it is for both sides in making informed decisions about how to move forward. By sharing and discovering all relevant information, I mean that you need to explore and communicate:

❖ How both parties feel.
❖ How both parties see the key issues.
❖ How you, the other person or outside influences have contributed to the issue.
❖ Both parties' intentions.
❖ Concerns or fears.
❖ What each person wants or needs.

You can help the other person into a more receptive state by authentic attentive listening. You can move farther towards a safe and productive dialogue with the following strategies:

❖ Use non-defensive language (explained on page 189).
❖ Share and acknowledge your feelings (explained on page 191).
❖ Disclose all relevant information, even that which doesn't necessarily support your desired outcome.

The final bullet point normally has my workshop delegates looking worried and confused. Being willing to share where you have contributed to a problem, divulging your truest motives or admitting where your version of the issues may be based more on assumption than on fact will open you up to potentially more questions and even criticism from the other person. Yet crucially, it also models to the other party your willingness to be transparent and honest. This builds trust that it's OK to be more open, increasing the chances that you will get more transparency and relevant information back from the other person.

This doesn't mean you allow the conversation to be a one-way street of honest dialogue. Let's look at an example where you're trying your best to look at the issues systemically and you want to surface both parties' contributions to the issue. Obviously, a good place to start is to build trust by sharing your inputs. But what if the other person either doesn't readily acknowledge their contribution or is genuinely blind to what they might or might have not done? In this situation you still have the right to say something like:

> "Sean, I've explained where I believe I've contributed to this issue, and I also believe there have been a couple of ways you have contributed. I'd like to share with you how I see that and then get your take on whether or not you see it the same way."

Notice that you're not being a doormat and taking all the responsibility, and yet you have also not gone into command and control. You remain in a mutual understanding, third-generation mindset, because you finish your sentence by letting Sean know that you want to know if he sees your view of his contributions differently.

"If I knew you and you knew me—
If both of us could clearly see,
And with an inner sight divine
The meaning of your heart and mine—
I'm sure that we would differ less
And clasp our hands in friendliness;
Our thoughts would pleasantly agree
If I knew you and you knew me."

Nixon Waterman

Identify individual and shared interests

Both parties have a range of hopes, fears and underlying needs that they are hoping to achieve or resolve by the end of the conversation. Often this leads to a battle between one person's objective and the other's. Such a battle either ends up with the conversation at a stalemate or one party defers to a rights- or power-based approach, where they try to enforce rules or policies, or use position or even intimidation to achieve their objective. In Chapter 12 I describe skills that when applied together can reduce the likelihood of your conversation ending up as a battle of wills.

Generate options

The success of this phase is highly reliant on how well you have explored your stories and understood and shared each other's underlying needs and concerns. If these two stages have been done well, there should now be some fertile ground of trust and understanding. Now you have earned the right to partner with the other person in generating a range of possible options or ways forward that will meet both parties' underlying interests.

When brainstorming ways forward, you may find that some options are not favourable to either person. When this occurs I simply fall back on sharing my concerns and look for other options that work for both parties.

In certain difficult conversations where the focus is on giving bad news, the main focus is unlikely to be on generating options. Chapter 14 is devoted specifically to delivering difficult messages.

Agree on specific next steps

In my experience of observing people engaged in difficult conversations, if the two parties have got to this stage they are generally feeling open and relaxed, having had their issues and feelings aired and acknowledged. They also see the other person in a more favourable light and may even be excited by the options and solutions that have been discussed. When I'm mediating it's at this point that the two parties ideally want to shake hands and move on with their lives. I then remind them that we haven't actually agreed on who will do what and when, and how we will know if something is working.

If you do not leave the table with a clear, mutual understanding of agreements, expectations and actions, invariably a mixture of misunderstandings and perceived broken promises can obliterate all the previous good work. Even worse, a sense of scepticism can grow around the benefit of investing so much time and emotional energy in these significant and challenging conversations. This area deserves attention, and again, there are specific skills for this in Chapter 12.

12
Skills for Vital Conversations

This chapter outlines seven skills that you can apply to your vital conversations. There are case studies or examples of how each skill can be used and how the tools link back to key areas of your vital conversation preparation.

Let's take another look at the model we first looked at in Chapter 10, page 154. As a quick reminder, your goal is to create a pot of mutual understanding by explaining both stories, before identifying key interests and generating options and next steps. As you can see from the diagram below, I have now added the seven skills to the model, which can be applied like a Swiss army knife to any part of the conversation you find yourself in.

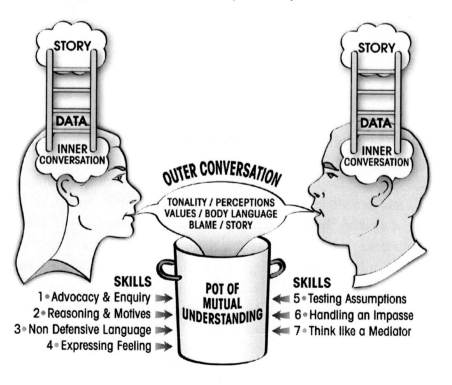

STORY

STORY

DATA

DATA

INNER CONVERSATION

INNER CONVERSATION

OUTER CONVERSATION

TONALITY / PERCEPTIONS
VALUES / BODY LANGUAGE
BLAME / STORY

SKILLS
1 • Advocacy & Enquiry ➡
2 • Reasoning & Motives ➡
3 • Non Defensive Language ➡
4 • Expressing Feeling ➡

POT OF MUTUAL UNDERSTANDING

SKILLS
⬅ 5 • Testing Assumptions
⬅ 6 • Handling an Impasse
⬅ 7 • Think like a Mediator

The first two skills need to be combined to maximise their effectiveness. Curiosity is the foundation behind them.

Skill 1: Blend advocacy with pure enquiry

"It takes courage to stand up and speak, as well as to sit down and listen."   *Anonymous*

In layperson's terms, advocacy is simply sharing your point of view and enquiry is attempting to see how other people see things, and encouraging the other person to clarify or question your own point of view.

The blending aspect is a crucial factor here. When you only advocate your point of view the other person can feel that you don't care about how they see things. If you hog the air time you also don't get to hear their perspective, needs and feelings, and therefore there are blank spaces in the shared pot of mutual under-standing (see the diagram on the previous page). On the other hand, if you are only enquiring then the other person doesn't understand what you're thinking and may become defensive in the face of a barrage of questions.

Skill 2: Make your reasoning and motives explicit

To make the tool of advocacy and genuine enquiry effective and safe in a vital conversation, you need to combine it with the skill of making both your reasoning and your motives explicit. In essence, this means that you share your thinking and intentions behind either advocating a point of view or asking a question.

Here is a classic example I see when a senior management team are discussing a key operational decision. The marketing director might advocate as follows:

"We must act now to improve the quality control on the assembly line, as we have to reduce the number of customer complaints from defective products."

There are two opportunities for significant misunderstanding here. First, he hasn't shared his reasoning or the motives behind his point of view. We are story-making animals and are all subject to the ladder of inference. In this example other directors will simply fill in the gaps in information that the marketing director has not provided with their own assumptions, many of which may be incorrect. The manufacturing director might see the marketing director's comments as an attack on his business unit. It would be very easy for him to race up his ladder and either quietly seethe or come back with some defensive remarks.

Secondly, the marketing director did not follow up his point of view by inquiring whether any of his peers saw things differently. If nobody responds then he may assume (potentially incorrectly) that everybody agrees with him. Several weeks later at a subsequent board meeting, he may become highly frustrated as the manufacturing director, who did not buy into his point of view, has done nothing to improve assembly-line quality.

Here is one way the marketing director could have shared the reasoning and intent behind his point of view while including some enquiry:

"I believe that we must act now to improve the quality control on the assembly line, as we have to reduce the number of customer complaints about defective products. Let me share with you how I arrived at this conclusion. Sales have risen far quicker than expected and Clare's production team in my opinion have been overworked and understaffed for several months. If customer complaints continue to rise at their current levels, we will have a tipping point where our customers no longer believe that we can be trusted, therefore creating long-term damage to the brand. I'd like to know if any of you see this differently or if you could shed light on anything I've missed or overlooked."

Because he is making all his thinking transparent, the other directors have a much more complete picture. Of course, it doesn't guarantee that another director won't respond defensively, but the extra relevant information does reduce the potential for the ladder effect and his enquiry at the end invites collaboration, openness and further debate.

The diagram below represents a helicopter view of how to advocate or enquire while also sharing your reasoning and intent.

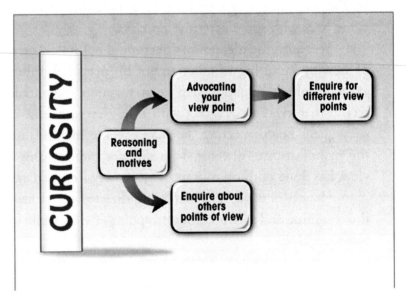

Once more, the key to benefiting from these skills comes from being curious. If you operate from the third-generation assumptions that you can't possibly have all the information and that the other person could be perceiving certain aspects differently, you will naturally share more of the thinking behind your point of view and questions.

It's really a question of deciding whether you feel it's more appropriate to explain your reasoning and intent before you advocate/enquire or whether you place it after you have made your point or asked a question.

Key learn: Always keep in mind that if you have made a significant point or expressed a bold view, always add a checking question to give the other person a chance to respond. An example would be, "Do you see anything I've just said differently?"

Tainted versus pure enquiry

Enquiry questions are not always what they seem; sometimes they are used in an indirect way to disguise a point of view. People often hide their true thoughts, wants and feelings behind questions. You may also use questions as a way of avoiding making a direct statement and therefore having to take taking ownership of what you have just said.

If you're asking what I would call a pure enquiry question, your intention behind the question is only to discover or clarify something. You will also be genuinely open and curious to what the person responds with. Tainted enquiry questions are those that are phrased as a question but actually contain some subliminal advocacy. Here are a few examples:

Tainted enquiry	What they are really thinking but not saying
"Don't you think it would be better if you did it this way?"	"I think it would be better if you did it this way"
"Are we going to spend all day talking about this one issue?"	"I'm frustrated and want to discuss other issues."

Think carefully about the questions you are about to ask. Are they really questions or disguised ways of saying things that you are uncomfortable being transparent about? Remember, if you are uncomfortable making a point directly, you can always share your reasoning and intent behind it. People will then understand why you're conveying such an important or challenging view.

Enquiry is at the heart of understanding their story

"People don't care how much you know – until they know how much you care."   *John C. Maxwell*

If you want the other person to listen to you, nine times out of ten you are the one who's going to have to role model that behaviour first. By now you have already evolved into the third-generation mindset and you are naturally curious to find out how the other person sees things. However, here are some guidelines for exploring their story:

❖ Most people have a strong psychological need for understanding, so where appropriate and having established why you're both having the conversation, encourage the other person to share first: "I'm curious to get your take on how we have arrived at this situation."

❖ Respectfully acknowledge any feelings without necessarily having to agree with them: "I'm guessing that you are frustrated to find out that the job was offered to an external candidate and not you."

❖ Paraphrase key aspects of what the other person has divulged, especially those aspects about which they have been most passionate or concerned. For example, a parent might say to their teenage daughter: "I can see that you want to be able to stay out later at weekends and that you really want me to have more faith and trust in your ability to say safe and responsible. Have I missed anything here?" Notice that the parent doesn't agree or disagree, merely mirrors what is important to their daughter.

❖ Dig deeper into how they see and feel about things by using simple but highly powerful enquiry questions: "You mentioned impossible workload and deadlines. Can you tell me a little more about that?"

❖ Remember to share your reasoning and intent behind some of your enquiry, as people start to get defensive if they don't know why you're asking questions: "I want to find out more about your concerns regarding deadlines and workloads because..."

❖ Finally, remember that you don't necessarily have to agree with the viewpoints, perceptions, values or rules that are being expressed; your goal is to understand them. Psychological research into empathy shows that people are more positively moved by someone who is trying to understand them than by someone who can accurately guess how they are feeling. That is, the state of the relationship benefits as much from the intention to understand than from the understanding itself. With courage and skill, you will still have your opportunity to share how you see things and then find a mutually beneficial path forward.

Reticent story tellers

There may well be occasions when you engage in a vital conversation and the other person is reluctant to talk. Here are some of the reasons this might happen:

❖ The other person is afraid of you or does not trust you enough to talk. If this is the case, you may need several attempts at the conversation to show that you really do care before they begin to open up.

❖ It's possible that they have become so emotional that it's simply too hard for them to talk or they are worried that if they start, the tears or anger might not stop. If you sense that they are becoming overwhelmed, if at all possible take time out or reschedule the conversation, giving them time to work through their feelings.

❖ The issues may be particularly raw and hard for them to talk about and they may find it difficult to know where to start.

If you sense that the other person is not overwhelmed but at the same time they are sharing very little in response to your advocacy, it may be worth trying some very tentative inquiry. The idea behind this is a bit like rolling a snowball down a hill. At first you have to put some effort into getting the ball moving, but after a while it gains its own momentum, picking up more snow as it goes. When you're only getting short or yes/no answers to your questions, then reaching into their story with gentle enquiry can sometimes get the conversational snowball rolling.

Start by mentally standing in the other person's shoes and making your best guess about:

❖ How they are feeling right now.
❖ What's bothering them most.
❖ What you feel may be most important to them at that moment.

For example, "I'm wondering if you have some concerns about sharing your views on the situation because you're afraid the conversation may not remain confidential."

Real-life case study: Getting the snowball rolling

About two years ago I was running a workshop for IT consultants from a well-known blue-chip company. Within 40 minutes of starting I sensed a severe reluctance from the group to connect with the learning and insights I was sharing. I asked some enquiry questions and also shared my reasons for doing so:

"I just want to get some feedback from the group on whether my approach and material are working for you. I'm asking this because I'm a little confused. Usually by now delegates are getting some real benefit from the course and the amount of questions I receive would be significantly higher than what I'm receiving today. Could you let me know what's going on for you?"

For some trainers even doing this would be too risky. What if they came back and said they were finding the workshop patronising and unchallenging? I'm not sure any coach or trainer would want to hear that, but at least I would have had more data to understand where to go next.

What I actually received, other than a couple of comments that "it's fine", was zero feedback. After 12 years running workshops in the corporate world, I do have some experience of why groups are unwilling to open up to learning. I decided that it was worth testing my hypothesis with some advocacy. I asked tentatively:

> "I may be way off track here, but is anyone frustrated or resentful about being sent on a course that you knew little or nothing about? In fact, I'm wondering if anyone has experienced feeling patronised or controlled by being told that you needed to attend this workshop?"

Still nothing, so I went on.

> "Over the years I've encountered situations where the way in which people have been told to attend training courses has left a lot to be desired. I genuinely would like to find out what your experience has been so that we can make the best of whatever we decide to do going forward. Are my assumptions about how you're feeling accurate?"

There was silence for about another 10 seconds (it felt like 30 minutes), then one man spoke up:

> "HR do whatever they please, they never consult us and we just get a three-line whip from our bosses. We already spend too much time on the road away from our families and this is just another two days away from home."

This opened the flood gates. As other people gained confidence in voicing their irritations, the snowball was off and rolling. Having explored their story and acknowledged their frustrations, I shared my feelings, concerns and hopes for the course. We jointly agreed what aspects would be most useful for their roles and how best to organise the rest of the workshop. As time away from home was a big issue, I committed to ending the workshop after lunch the next day, giving everyone the chance to get back home before 5.30 p.m. The IT company did not get the full version of the workshop on that occasion, but it did get a group of delegates who became engaged and in fact highly committed to the aspects of the learning they had agreed to. This feedback also became invaluable in talking with their HR department and changing the way in which workshop attendance was communicated to future delegates.

Practising advocacy and pure enquiry

In some respects you need both to break old habits and to learn a new language. If your habitual approach to high-stakes conversations has been win/lose, then increasing the number of pure enquiry questions you ask feels awkward. In contrast, if your style has been to compromise or accommodate other people's needs, you may well be uncomfortable advocating what's most important to you.

Opposite and overleaf are two diagrammatic representations of how to improve your advocacy and enquiry. It's important to note that this is my style of language and you may have to adapt the words used to fit your personality and background. Just remember to remove any doubt in the other person's mind about why you are advocating or enquiring by sharing your reasoning and motives.

Mini exercise: Practise not advocating!

One of the best ways to improve your capacity to listen is to refrain from giving your opinion. In low-stakes conversations or where it's not essential for you to have an input, make a conscious effort simply to listen. You may also want to ask a few "pure" inquiry questions. Remain aware of how the other person responds. They may relax more as their need for understanding is met; they may even seek your opinion as subconsciously they sense that you are not seeking to impose your view on them. Don't be surprised if practising not needing to convey an opinion does wonders for some of your most important relationships!

Enhancing advocacy

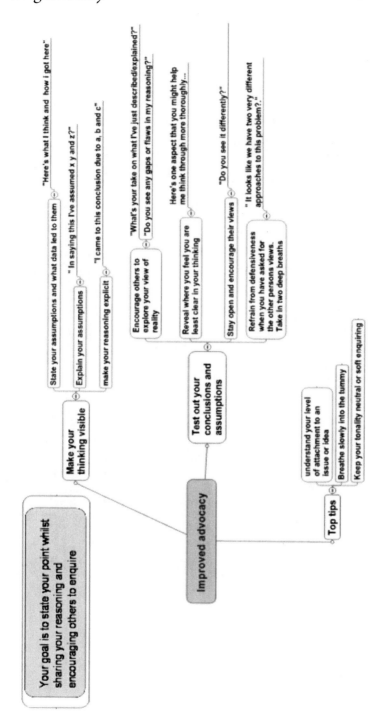

Your goal is to state your point whilst sharing your reasoning and encouraging others to enquire

Improved advocacy

Make your thinking visible

State your assumptions and what data led to them — "Here's what I think and how I got here"

Explain your assumptions — "In saying this I've assumed x y and z?"

make your reasoning explicit — "I came to this conclusion due to a, b and c"

Test out your conclusions and assumptions

Encourage others to explore your view of reality — "What's your take on what I've just described/explained?" "Do you see any gaps or flaws in my reasoning?"

Reveal where you feel you are least clear in your thinking — Here's one aspect that you might help me think through more thoroughly....

Stay open and encourage their views — "Do you see it differently?"

Refrain from defensiveness when you have asked for the other persons views. Take in two deep breaths — "It looks like we have two very different approaches to this problem?"

Top tips

understand your level of attachment to an issue or idea

Breathe slowly into the tummy

Keep your tonality neutral or soft enquiring

Enhancing enquiry

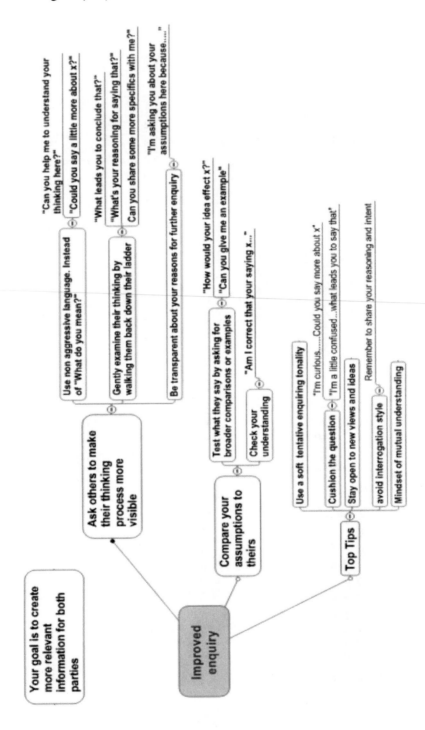

Your goal is to create more relevant information for both parties

Improved enquiry

Ask others to make their thinking process more visible

Use non aggressive language. Instead of "What do you mean?"
- "Can you help me to understand your thinking here?"
- "Could you say a little more about x?"

Gently examine their thinking by walking them back down their ladder
- "What leads you to conclude that?"
- "What's your reasoning for saying that?"
- Can you share some more specifics with me?"

Be transparent about your reasons for further enquiry
- "I'm asking you about your assumptions here because....."

Compare your assumptions to theirs

Test what they say by asking for broader comparisons or examples
- "How would your idea effect x?"
- "Can you give me an example"

Check your understanding
- "Am I correct that your saying x..."

Top Tips

Use a soft tentative enquiring tonality

Cushion the question
- "I'm curious......Could you say more about x"
- "I'm a little confused....what leads you to say that"

Stay open to new views and ideas

avoid interrogation style

Mindset of mutual understanding

Remember to share your reasoning and intent

Skill 3: Non-defensive language

"In quarrelling the truth is always lost."

Publilius Syrus

When you're engaged in a vital yet difficult conversation, the stress levels encountered by both parties will be significantly higher than in everyday conversations, and if there is historical baggage the tension will be even more acute. Selecting what you say and how you say it is critical to keeping the conversation on the rails. Sometimes it takes only a word, a judgemental statement or a critical tone to put the conversation into a flat spin from which it's very hard to recover.

I will first raise your awareness of "landmine language" that can blow up productive dialogue and then move on to look at how a mediator uses non-defensive language to minimise negative reactions from the other person.

Landmine dialogue

Let's remind ourselves once more of the components of a vital conversation: high stakes, differing opinions, historical baggage, uncertainty and powerful emotions. It's no wonder that some of the most destructive communication can happen given this combination of pressures.

Having prepared thoroughly using the vital conversations coaching tool and used and practised the emotional state management techniques described in this book, I'm hoping that you can minimise or ideally remove all of the following landmine language from your dialogue under stress:

❖ *Blaming*: "If you hadn't messed up the dates we wouldn't have missed that meeting with our most important client."
❖ *"I'm not saying" statements*: "I'm not saying you lied but", "I'm not saying you did it on purpose but", "I'm not saying you're

the only one who's responsible but" (a disguised way of saying you did lie, did do it on purpose or are solely responsible).

❖ *Moralistic judgements*: "If you weren't so lazy, insensitive, controlling" (all these attack the other person's very identity, causing hurt and defensive reactions).

❖ *Guilt tripping*: "You have really let both me and your father down and you've made us sad and disappointed" (this often works but you will pay a heavy price for using it).

❖ *Threatening or intimidating*: "You undermine my authority in a meeting one more time and..."

❖ *Sarcasm*: "Which part of the word 'no' don't you understand?" or "Yeah, right."

❖ *Reclaiming baggage*: "You've missed important deadlines before, remember the time when you..."

❖ *Putting a negative spin on what they said*: "What you really think is..." or "What you're actually saying is..."

❖ *Generalising*: "You always have to get your own way."

❖ *Exaggerating*: "You're going to tear this family apart."

❖ *Accusations of bad intent*: "Sometimes you start these fights on purpose" or "Do you get pleasure from embarrassing me in front of your family?"

❖ *Negating feelings*: "Don't you think you're overreacting?" or "Calm down."

❖ *Making remarks about the other person's capability*: "You just don't make any sense" or "It's like talking to a brick wall."

"Sharp words make more wounds than surgeons can heal."

Anonymous

Tone and body language

People say a picture is worth a thousand words and it's the same with your body language. If the position of your arms and torso reeks of frustration, that negative energy will transfer to the other person. Unfortunately, because you are not managing or verbally communicating your current state of frustration, it's likely that the other person will race up their mental ladder and start making unproductive assumptions about your demeanour.

To understand the impact of tone, have a go at saying the following sentence. First say it with a bland, neutral tone and then say it several times, but each time place a heavy emphasis on one of the words underlined.

"I never said <u>he</u> <u>stole</u> the <u>money</u>."

If you placed heavy emphasis on the word "he", the other person might come back and say, "So who did steal the money?" Alternatively, if you placed more emphasis on "money", the other person might respond, "So what did he steal?"

It's not easy to get this across in writing, but your tone can completely shift the meaning of your conversation. Even a short response like "I suppose so" can convey curiosity, resignation or scepticism about what the other person has said, simply by the tone that's added to the words.

When you're stressed it's very easy for your emotions to leak out in your tone. If you manage your emotional state you have more control over the tone you add to your words. There may well be times when you want to let the other person know that you're sad, shocked or surprised and if you're self-aware you can still convey those important feelings without lacing your words with a toxic tone that may provoke a defensive reaction.

Skill 4: Expressing how you feel

Sometimes feelings are just one aspect of a vital conversation and at other times they are central to it. When I mediate, as part of the process I ask each party to share how they see the current issues. As each person has their opportunity to talk, you can see in their body language, tone and the words they use that strong feelings bubbling under the surface are desperately trying to be aired and acknowledged.

Nobody has a monopoly on feelings and you and the person you're in dialogue with should be allowed to express your emotions. There may be valid reasons why you might not want to share certain feelings, but be warned: if you find that your reason for not sharing sounds something like "I don't want to make a mountain out of a molehill" or "They will only get mad or worry" or the all-time classic "It's really not that important", you may well be consistently negating your own feelings. This can have the following consequences:

❖ You teach people how to treat you.
❖ Buried feelings leak out into the conversation.
❖ You eventually explode or implode.

Real-life case study: I want to be alone

Jan's father, who lives close by, often comes over to Jan's house unannounced for a coffee and a catch-up. Jan loves her dad, but these unscheduled visits and the time it takes to make coffee and listen to her father's woes play havoc with her workload as a mum with three kids and a husband who works away a lot. Jan is often frustrated and is even becoming resentful of her dad's intrusions, but she also knows that since her mum died three years previously, her dad has found it hard to adjust to life on his own and gets lonely and bored. So Jan swallows her feelings and says nothing.

When Jan puts her dad's feelings ahead of her own and says nothing, she is teaching her dad how to treat her. The very act of passivity lets her dad know that Jan will stop what she is doing and make him the priority.

As Jan's resentment builds, she finds it harder and harder to listen to her dad and becomes less patient with her dad's concerns about being on his own. Unconsciously, Jan's dad feels this increasing disconnection and starts staying for longer or coming over more frequently as his needs for connection and emotional support are not met.

Jan will either explode or implode. If her father knocks at the door at a really stressful moment, Jan may tell him that he needs to get his own life and stop being so dependent on his children. She would later feel incredibly guilty at the way she spoke to her dad and go round to apologise, but she still wouldn't be tackling the issue. Alternatively, Jan may implode and become depressed, sick or numb to her father's ramblings. Whichever happens, she will be paying a heavy price for not being authentic about her feelings.

Misrepresenting feelings

Sometimes the challenge you face is that you do not have the awareness or emotional vocabulary to identify and share your feelings accurately with the other person. Marshall Rosenberg gives a great example in his book *NVC: The Language of Life*. A university student on one of his workshops spoke about a housemate who played music so loudly it kept him awake. When asked to express what he was feeling, the student replied, "I feel it isn't right to play music so loud at night." Marshall pointed out that when he followed the word "feel" with "it isn't right to play music so loudly at night", he was expressing an opinion and not a feeling. Asked to try again, the student responded, "I feel when people do something like that it's a personality disturbance." Marshall explained that this was still an opinion rather than a feeling. The student paused thoughtfully, and then announced with vehemence, "I have no feelings about this whatsoever!"

Most people have received very little training on accurately observing, sharing and taking ownership of their feelings. Across 15 years of school and college education, I can't recall a time that a teacher ever asked me how I was feeling. On my workshops I encourage people to practise explaining how they're feeling. Although I take great care to explain how to express feelings in a conversation, habitual ways of talking surface (especially under role-play pressures) and people tend to describe feelings in terms of how the other person is behaving rather than what they are feeling themselves.

Below are some common misrepresentations of feelings.

Diagnosis of what the other person is doing to you

> "I feel you are manipulating me."

Here you are possibly feeling frustrated or angry due to the other person's behaviour. This is a diagnosis of what the other person is doing rather than an actual feeling. You may be thinking that saying that isn't a big deal, but put yourself in the receiver's shoes. Would you find it easy to hear that you are manipulating someone? You may want to defend your behaviour and disagree with their diagnosis of your dubious character, or you may end up feeling hurt that someone thinks of you that way. Either way, it is unlikely to lead to a productive dialogue.

Judgements about the other person

> "I feel you are ignorant of current market trends."

Instead of this, I would ask you to be specific about the actual feeling and express it something like:

> "I'm feeling anxious when I hear you focus only on the manufacturing aspects and not take into account current market trends."

This would be even more effective if some of the other skills mentioned in this chapter were also used. For example, it would be useful if you added an enquiry question at the end:

> "I'm feeling anxious when I hear you focus only on the manufacturing aspects and not take into account current market trends. Have I missed anything here that might change the way I feel about this?"

Lack of self-ownership

> "You make me upset when you don't tidy up after yourself in the kitchen."

This only mentions the actions of the other person and can create defensiveness, as they either think they are being blamed or made responsible for your feelings. Instead, I advise you to own your emotion and describe how the behaviour and actions have affected you:

> "I feel upset when I see these unwashed dishes. My understanding was you had agreed to do these after dinner and that you would be more proactive round the house now that I am working full time as well. Could you give me your thoughts on what I've just said?"

If you are expressing feelings transparently, you often need to share more of the reasoning and intent (Skill 2) behind why you are conveying your feelings. And once more you need to enquire (Skill 1) to gain the other person's view of what you have just said, as they may see the situation differently or have information, perceptions and values of which you are not aware.

Guilt projection

> "You make mummy/daddy sad when you don't clean your room, get good grades, tell the truth, do your chores etc."

I see countless examples of people misrepresenting the language of feelings, but nowhere is this more sad and damaging to the long-term relationship than between parents and children. Over time your children may fall in line and do as you ask, but they don't do it out of love, they do it to avoid feeling guilty. Is that the basis for a loving, trusting relationship? I don't think so.

Taking ownership

When you take ownership of your feelings you gain several benefits. First, you become the master of your emotions rather than a
servant. From this place you can choose to share your feelings in
the conversation where appropriate. Secondly, when you show
others that you own and are willing to take responsibility for how
you feel, they are less likely to become defensive, as you are not
blaming your negative emotions on them. Finally, most people are
sensitive to how others feel and will have more empathy for your
situation.

Top tips: Getting feelings into your vital conversation

❖ Make sure that you're clear about which feelings you want
to convey. After you've read the rest of these tips, have a go
at writing out how you might actually include those feelings in
your conversation.

❖ If you're uncomfortable about sharing a feeling because of the potential impact it may have, then preface the feeling with your concern:
"It's hard for me to share how I'm feeling because I'm concerned that
it might make you defensive and yet I still want to let you know that I'm
feeling discouraged about..."

❖ It's OK to share conflicting feelings: "I'm frustrated that you don't want
to host the family Christmas this year as it's your turn. At the same
time I feel guilty for raising this with you, as I know December is always
the busiest time for your business and having the extra burden of a
family Christmas stresses you out."

❖ Express just the feeling without turning it into a moralistic judgement,
blame or diagnosis of what the other person has done.

❖ Take responsibility for your feelings by using "I" statements: "I'm confused when..."

❖ Share your reasoning and intentions when expressing powerful emotions. This will enable the other person to understand where your
strong feelings have come from and reduce the chances of them making inaccurate assumptions. "I'm feeling completely overwhelmed at
the moment. I really appreciate all the projects you have asked me to
take on, and I am very grateful that you have placed this level of trust
in me, but I'm afraid that I'm in danger of underperforming on at least

one of these new initiatives. Could you share with me your response to my telling you this?"
❖ Always try to close off your expression of a feeling by asking an enquiry question, as in the previous point.

Skill 5: Testing assumptions and mutual understanding

Research shows that even in a non-pressurised conversation, you only take in between 25 and 40% of what the other person is saying. If you consider the increased stress of a vital conversation, it's highly likely that one or both parties will be deleting or missing out on significant chunks of what the other person is conveying. Unfortunately, due to the pressure they are under and the need to make sense of what they are hearing, most people unconsciously fill in those gaps with their own thinking. To put it another way, they make assumptions.

In reality, you have to make assumptions all the time to be an effective and productive human being. There are many occasions where either you don't have all the data or you can't get all the information and so you have to make some assumptions and proceed on the basis of your best thinking at that time. Even in your vital conversations, you will need to make assumptions about what the other person is saying. That isn't a problem in itself. The challenge comes when you make critical assumptions about the person or the issues and treat them as the truth rather than an untested hypothesis about what the other person meant or intended.

Recall the ladder of inference, discussed on page 89. The diagram overleaf relates it to a vital conversation between Ingrid and Shaun, who are discussing whether their son should have a private or a state education.

In essence, the ladder shows how you take in data in terms of what the person is saying or doing, then create a story based on what you think you've heard. If the story has a negative outcome

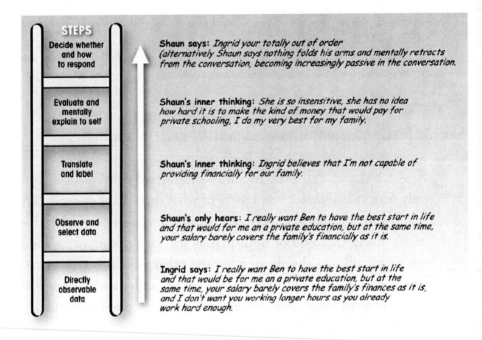

STEPS	
Decide whether and how to respond	**Shaun says:** *Ingrid your totally out of order (alternatively Shaun says nothing folds his arms and mentally retracts from the conversation, becoming increasingly passive in the conversation.*
Evaluate and mentally explain to self	**Shaun's inner thinking:** *She is so insensitive, she has no idea how hard it is to make the kind of money that would pay for private schooling, I do my very best for my family.*
Translate and label	**Shaun's inner thinking:** *Ingrid believes that I'm not capable of providing financially for our family.*
Observe and select data	**Shaun's only hears:** *I really want Ben to have the best start in life and that would for me an a private education, but at the same time, your salary barely covers the family's financially as it is.*
Directly observable data	**Ingrid says:** *I really want Ben to have the best start in life and that would be for me an a private education, but at the same time, your salary barely covers the family's finances as it is, and I don't want you working longer hours as you already work hard enough.*

Ladder of inference adapted from *The Skilled Facilitator*, © Roger Schwarz 2002. Reproduced with permission of Jossey Bass, Inc.

you generate unresourceful feelings, which help to make your assumptions feel real and therefore true in your mind. You then make some form of active or passive decision about how you are going to respond.

It's important to highlight that there are three subsets of assumptions that people commonly make when they move up their ladder.

Inferences

An inference is an assumption about something you don't know based on something you do. For example, you're walking in a park on a summer day and as you go over the brow of a hill you hear shouting and screaming, then you see two boys. The one who is two or three years older is sitting on top of the other one, pinning him down. From what you see you infer that one boy is hurting the other. You run over to intervene, only to find that they are brothers and are clearly mucking around and play fighting. You were correct that they were fighting, but your inference about the nature of their fighting was off the mark. In this scenario you went and checked out your inference, but in many challenging conversations people are not even aware of the inferences they are making and subsequently acting on.

Moralistic judgements

You may put your own judgemental spin on the inference you've drawn about someone's behaviour: "They're so inconsiderate, insensitive, bully, sexist, racist." These labels form the main image of how you see the person. Maybe not for ever, but certainly at that moment, everything they say and do is filtered through the label you have given them.

Attributions

You make an attribution when you take your assumptions about the other person's actions or decisions and begin to attribute complex or dubious motives. Attributing negative intentions is a conversational landmine for several reasons. The moment you add motive it makes the situation personal and it's not long before you shift to "They meant to do it". At this point your unresourceful feelings can sky rocket as you begin to see the person as the problem, rather than staying with the issues.

Going back to Ingrid and Shaun, at the bottom of the ladder you have Ingrid sharing what's important to her and giving her concerns about not wanting Shaun to work any harder. However, Shaun only hears the part about his wage only covering the monthly bills and no more. This is where he starts to make larger and larger jumps in mental abstraction, adding lots of his own private thinking to the words. In a matter of seconds he has inferred from his selective hearing that Ingrid believes he cannot provide for his family and then makes a moralistic judgement about her being insensitive.

Shaun now has to decide what to do. If he blurts out "That's really out of order", Ingrid may be shocked or surprised. If not handled carefully, the conversation could easily unravel. The real tragedy if this conversation then goes into meltdown is that both parents want the same outcome from the conversation – to work out how to support and provide for their son's education – but before they know it the conversation can become an argument full of hurt and defensiveness.

If Shaun decides to go quiet and become passive in the conversation, his private thinking will remain exactly that and Ingrid initially will have no idea that anything has been misinterpreted. As the conversation begins to become one way she may pick up on Shaun's passivity, but if she does not have the self-awareness or skills to inquire into the change of behaviour, she could race up her ladder and make inferences and attributions: "Shaun just doesn't seem interested, it's like getting blood out of a stone. I guess he just doesn't care about Ben's future. That's really irresponsible."

Testing your assumptions

Although testing assumptions is a challenging skill to learn, it is one of the most powerful and can be used in two helpful ways:

- ❖ To check on the assumptions and inferences you are making.
- ❖ To check on your intuition about the other person's potential assumptions and inferences.

Once again, your foundation is the third-generation mindset with curiosity at its core.

I will step into Shaun's shoes and highlight how I might test out his assumptions about what Ingrid has said:

Shaun hears: "I really want Ben to have the best start in life and that to me means providing him with a private education, but at the same time your salary barely covers the family's finances as it is."

Shaun's initial knee-jerk story is: "Ingrid believes that I'm not capable of providing financially for our family."

Step 1: Take a diaphragmatic slow breath and check on how you're feeling (in this case surprised and annoyed).

Step 2: Acknowledge your feeling so that it's been heard, as this will reduce its intensity ("I am feeling frustrated with Ingrid").

Step 3: Ask yourself "What's the story I'm telling here?" and remember that it's only an untested hypothesis until you have checked it out with the other person. In this case the story is "Ingrid believes that I'm not capable of providing financially for our family."

Step 4: Decide whether you want to check out your assumption with the other person. You can't check every assumption you make, as the conversation would take a week to have and you'd drive the other person crazy. However, if you are experiencing powerful emotions and your story is painting a negative picture about the other person or where this conversation is headed, then the chances are that you need to test out your assumption.

Step 5: Test out your assumption and check whether the other person agrees with you.

Be aware, though, that the higher you go up your ladder or the more abstract your thinking becomes, the harder it is to check out your inferences with the other person. For instance, if Shaun comes in with "Ingrid, you are so insensitive. Do you see that the same way?" he's probably not going to get a very useful response. I know that's an extreme example of going in high, but it should make the point. The goal is to make your inference as low on the ladder as possible, ideally going back to what you actually saw and heard and then sharing your inference without judgement or motive.

If I were Shaun I might test out the assumption in the following way:

> "Ingrid, I'd like to clarify something I just heard you say that I've had a strong reaction to. I heard you say that you really want Ben to have the best start in life and that would for you mean providing him with a private education, but at the same time you mentioned that the salary I bring in barely covers the family finances as it is. Did I hear that right?"

Notice that I included a checking question to make sure that he did hear Ingrid correctly. Let's assume that Ingrid says, "Yes, that's right."

This is how I would keep the inference I'm testing out as low as possible:

> "When I heard what you said, I initially felt surprised and annoyed because I was thinking that you were unhappy with my ability to provide enough money for what our family needs. Did I get that right or am I misunderstanding you?"

Notice again a checking question that is consistent with the third-generation approach of honouring that the other person might see things differently.

Based on what Ingrid actually said, it's highly likely that she would come back and say something like, "No, not at all. I really do value what you do and I did also say that I didn't want you working more hours. You do more than enough for this family already."

In that one moment Shaun has burst through his original story and created a broader understanding between himself and his wife. Of course, in a different situation she may have said, "I do have concerns over the amount of money you bring home for the family." In that case Shaun would need to use the Swiss army knife of skills in this chapter and begin to explore his wife's perceptions, feelings and the overall story behind her concerns. Remember, there are no easy vital conversations, but with these skills and the right mindset you can make them far more productive.

Testing their assumptions

You may be wondering how you test out the other person's assumptions if everything's going on in their mind. You're absolutely right: you cannot see into their private thoughts, but their private thoughts might show up in their body language, tone of voice or words.

Of course, if you're observing what you infer as defensive body language, you only have a hunch or a hypothesis, but if you sense that not checking it out would be detrimental to the success of the conversation, I would recommend doing so. Sometimes people give away a potential high-level story in their words. You may have witnessed someone respond with a sarcastic "Yeh, right". When this happens there's more than a 90% chance that they have reservations about what someone has just said, yet you'd be amazed how many people would not check on a response like that.

If "Yeh, right" came from one of my workshop delegates, I might test my assumption of their inference with:

"Ravi, I have a concern that you may have had a strong reaction to the point I just conveyed. Is my concern correct or am I off track here?"

Ravi may agree and immediately explain his concern, or I may need to enquire further:

"Could you give me your take on the point I made?"

Sometimes you read into the situation something that was never there. Alternatively, some people may not want to reveal their private thinking, yet the intent and curiosity you demonstrate to clarify your assumptions indicates your positive intention to try to understand what is important to them.

Reducing the number of assumptions

One of the best ways to reduce the dangers of untested assumptions is to share your reasoning (Skill 1) behind saying things. The more relevant information you provide when advocating a point of view or enquiring, the less likely the other person is to fill in the gaps with their own mental abstractions, most of which won't be helpful.

Skill 6: Handling an impasse

Sometimes you may do a great job of understanding the other person's story and sharing your own, only to find that they have a very fixed opinion of what needs to be done or the solution that should be put in place. Often that solution doesn't work for you or you may feel that their approach isn't necessarily the most effective use of your resources or time. Hopefully you have used the vital conversations coaching tool to work out your underlying interests behind your outcomes for the conversation, but the other person is unlikely to have done the same.

Positions versus interests

In the planning phase of your vital conversation, I covered the subject of positions versus interests. You will remember that a position is a single answer or solution to a problem, whereas interests are the needs, concerns or hopes that people have in a given situation. Positions tend to hide individual interests.

When you find that the other person is attached to a particular course of action, it can be helpful to adopt one of the following questions in your conversation:

❖ "What is most important to you about proceeding in this way?"

❖ "If we did decide to move forward in this way, what would it do for you or give you?"

You may find that the other person is not capable of giving an instant reply about their underlying interests or motivations, as most people build solutions to their problems with only a low level of awareness of their deeper needs.

The best way of showing how to employ this skill is with a case study. Remind yourself of the case of Samrah and Jalil on page 141, who want to book their annual summer holiday.

Case study: Understanding deeper interests

If I were to coach Samrah and Jalil with the questions above, these could be some of the answers:

COACH: "What would going to a 5-star beach resort do for you or give you?"

SAMRAH: "I'm really worn out right now, and a 5-star all-inclusive resort would mean I could totally relax and turn off my brain, no cooking or cleaning, somebody at my every beck and call. I also need to get away from having a schedule, my job is really busy and I just want some time out from doing, doing, doing!

COACH: What about you, Jalil, what's important to you?

JALIL: Well, my job isn't that demanding and I want to be challenged, to discover or learn new things. I also want to have that wonderful physically tired feeling that you get at the end of the day when you've really exercised hard.

If I was to succinctly summarise their deeper interests, I'd say that Samrah's are for relaxation, switch-off time and autonomy from commitments and Jalil wants learning, adventure and a physical stretch.

Once you understand both parties' interests, there are many possible holiday destinations that meet all their needs. Provided that Samrah gets 5-star pampering, does she really need to be at a beach-only resort? Provided that Jalil gets his needs for adventure and exercise met, could they find an up-market beach resort that specialises in outdoor activities?

Top tip: Chunking up

Sometimes you reach an impasse in a conversation where neither side can agree on how to move forward, the conversation gets bogged down in detail and people get frustrated. At these moments it can be helpful to use a technique called chunking up. In essence, you get the other person's attention, explain your concerns about the lack of progress and express your genuine intention to try to get the conversation moving again. The question you then ask both them and you at the same time is:

"What can we agree is most important for both of us here?"
Or "Ultimately what are we both trying to achieve?"

It may be that the question is directed more at the issue or situation you're talking about:

"What's most important for our ongoing business partnership in all this?"

These questions encourage both parties to chunk up their thinking to a common cause or to what is most important.

Real-life case study: Rising above the ego

I remember when our son was only six months old and suffering from reflux, a painful condition of the stomach that leaves the baby in a lot of pain. Two sleep-deprived parents were trying to discuss how we handled feeding times (which most aggravated his condition). The conversation quickly turned into an argument as Gill and I began to get frustrated with each other's differing solutions.

It was she who took a deep breath and said, "Stop! This is going nowhere. What's most important here?"

We soon realised that it was our little boy who was in a lot of pain, and as two adults it was imperative that we put our egos to one side and cracked on as a team to reduce his suffering. That two-second intervention from Gill was transformative as we rallied to a common cause.

Skill 7: Thinking like a mediator

"It takes two to make a quarrel but only one to end it."
Spanish proverb

Your upcoming vital conversation may of course be with an expert in conflict resolution, but if that isn't the case you may experience one or more of the following:

❖ You listen and explore and they have verbal incontinence.
❖ You acknowledge their feelings, they trample all over yours.
❖ You admit your mistakes, they confirm your mistakes and then deny any responsibility.
❖ You share your interests, they ram a solution down your throat.

Sound unfair? It probably is, but what are your options? You could say that the other person should be more mature and open, but as expert in self-enquiry Byron Katie says, "When you argue with reality, reality wins, but only 100% of the time." If the reality is that the other person communicates in ways that are not useful, then that's what you have to deal with. You could walk away from having the conversation, but then the problem usually gets worse and the relationship deteriorates.

I'm going to make the assumption that if you have come this far, you are going to have the conversation. If that's the case, you are going to have to take the overall lead on keeping it on the rails. At times in the conversation the road will get rocky, and in these moments I would recommend that you think like a mediator. There are three mediation skills you can employ to keep the conversation safe and productive.

Reframing
Reframing is the process of changing the way a thought is communicated so that it maintains its fundamental meaning but is

more likely to support productive dialogue. A large part of a mediator's role is to act like a translator. For instance, when Party A blames Party B, the mediator will reword what was said in terms of how Party A believes that Party B has contributed to the situation. In essence it's the same meaning, yet Party B has a significantly higher chance of being able to listen to the translated version without becoming defensive.

You can reframe almost anything. Here is an example of a father reframing his daughter's words on how she views his intentions. The 16-year-old daughter wants to camp at a rock festival for the weekend with friends and the father has said no.

DAUGHTER: I hate you! What is it with you? All my friends' parents think it's fine. Why do you have this need to ruin my life?

COMMON RESPONSE FROM THE FATHER: I'm not anyone else's parent, I'm yours, and I'm not trying to ruin your life. For God's sake stop overreacting. There will be plenty of other rock concerts when you're old enough.

DAUGHTER'S WORDS REFRAMED BY THE FATHER: I can see you're angry with my decision, and I do understand that this time with your friends is really important to you. It also sounds like you believe I'm making decisions that are restricting the kind of experiences you want to have. At the same time, I have some real concerns over your safety and on this occasion I need to place your safety higher than you enjoying new experiences with your friends. Could you give me your take on what I just said?

There is a lot more conversation that needs to be had and the daughter will still in all likelihood have a sense of resentment, but the parent has managed to reframe the daughter's words to demonstrate to her that he understands her frustration, but in a way that reframes the inflammatory dialogue.

So when someone says "You're the one who screwed this up" (having taken a deep breath and in your mind thought "Fascinating behaviour!") a potential reframing might be: "There are some things I have done that have led to where we find ourselves today and I believe we need to discuss where we have both contributed."

Alternatively, sometimes the other person will put an amazing spin on what you have just said. Imagine you're in a conversation with your partner and you are requesting that you would like to have more time where you do your own thing without them.

They say, "So you're getting bored with my company" (you didn't say or mean this).

You reframe this as, "It seems like you have some concerns over whether I enjoy your companionship. In fact that was the last thing on my mind, I love being with you. What I do think, though, is that it's healthy in a relationship to have some space from each other. From time to time I need to do some activities on my own or with other friends."

Reframing is not an easy skill to master. It takes a lot of curiosity and compassion to see through the toxic words and a lot of brain power to find alternatives that still speak to the person's underlying needs, concerns, hopes and fears. Yet the effort is worth it, as this is one of the most powerful skills for keeping your vital conversation on a positive track.

Using "and" to honour differences and still state what's important to you

The "and" stance was pioneered by the seminal work of the Harvard Negotiation Project and became widely understood after the release of the acclaimed bestseller *Getting to Yes* by Roger Fisher, William Ury and Bruce Patton.

There will be times when the two parties to the conversation have very fixed opinions about how they see things and it is unlikely that your thinking is going to meet in the middle. In these moments it is easy to feel that you have to either accept or reject the other person's story, and that if you accept theirs you have to let go of yours. The "and" stance allows you to respect both parties' differences of opinion *and* still get across what's most important to you.

Real-life case study: The family business

Jacob is in a difficult conversation with his dad. His father, a self-made millionaire, does not see the relevance of his son going to university and wants him to go into the family business with a view to taking over as managing director when he retires.

This is how Jacob uses the "and" stance to respect both opinions and still have the conviction to stay true to his own life path:

> "Dad, I can see how much it would mean to you if I took over the business, **and** that you are frustrated and disappointed, **and** I'm touched that you have the faith and trust in me that I could one day run the whole show **and** I also know that I want to experience a different lifestyle, meet new people and gain a deep understanding of a subject I love, therefore I'm still choosing to go to university."

Dealing with an explosion

Sometimes the other person shouts and explodes; at other times they stay silent or cry. If you're not used to dealing with conflict, either reaction can be disconcerting. The steps to follow are:

1. *Centre yourself.* Take several deep diaphragmatic breaths, as explained on page 101. This helps you regain your mental balance and remain calm yet focused.

2. *Acknowledge your feelings.* Recognise your own feelings as valid and remind yourself that you do not need to take ownership for the way they are feeling, although what you have said or done may have been a stimulus for those feelings.

3. *Let the observer in you become curious and empathetic.* Imagine that your higher intelligence has floated to the side and upwards to gain a unique and more detached viewpoint on the situation. From that vantage point, become curious about what must be going on for the other person. Your inner dialogue drives your inner stories, so focusing your inner voice on questions or statements like "This person looks to be really hurting" or "What needs to happen for them to be able to continue with this conversation?" or "I wonder what's driving such an angry

response?" will help you focus on the human being behind the behaviour.

4. *Acknowledge what's happening for the other person.* If they have gone on the offensive, it's likely that their dialogue is being driven by emotion – and emotion has a tendency to maintain momentum until it's acknowledged. I recommend you make an educated guess about the other person's feelings. The challenge is to do this without coming across as making assumptions about those emotions. People tend to get defensive when they're told they must be feeling a particular way. Check out your gut instinct by using a tentative tone, where the pitch of your voice rises at the end of the sentence. This turns a statement into a question and makes your guess less presumptuous. You may say, "I'm thinking that you're feeling very frustrated." Try that statement now out loud or in your head, increasing your pitch on the word "frustrated", and you should hear how the statement sounds more like a question. It's possible that your guess has missed the mark and that's not how they're feeling, but in my experience the very worst that happens is that the other person says no and then usually shares with me how they are feeling. If you guess right, at some level (usually subconscious) the other person acknowledges the empathy you're attempting to show them and the emotional intensity lowers a notch or two.

5. *Give them space.* Finally, give the other person space to talk and verbalise their feelings. If you rush them into talking before they have had a chance to process their strong feelings, you are only going to come up against more defensive energy when you try to explore options and ways forward.

Now that you have the skills to conduct a productive and effective vital conversation, the next chapter looks at how to bring that conversation to an appropriate end.

13
Ending the Conversation

The way you conclude a vital conversation is as important as the way you start it. Having done the hard work of creating a shared reservoir of joint understanding and discussed mutually beneficial options, it's too easy to fall into the trap of thinking that now you've had a really constructive conversation, everything's going to be fine. Not nearly enough time is given to this final phase and you and the other person part with vague next steps and too many untested assumptions.

It's crucial not just to get specific and accountable, but also to clarify what might prevent one of you from doing what you've agreed. This chapter descibes a simple five-step approach to gaining watertight clarity on the next steps, called the 5Ws.

1 Who is responsible?

Many people aren't comfortable making direct requests of others and therefore use statements like "We urgently need to get this done by next Wednesday". But which party do you mean by "we" and are you going to wait until 5 p.m. on Wednesday to find out that they thought or hoped it was you? Make sure you agree who's accountable for each action. Let's face it, when you're direct and specific the worst that can happen is that the other person says that they don't agree, and at least then you know where you stand.

2 What specifically is the other person agreeing to do?

Here you need to clarify not just what action is to be completed, but how it is to be done. Once again, you can hold hidden or implicit rules that come into play around standards or behaviour in the way the agreed action is carried out. It may be that once you describe your expectations to the other person they may not want to agree to the action or change in behaviour, but at least you've identified a potential misunderstanding at that point, rather than in three weeks' time when it will be ten times more frustrating or costly.

Real-life case study: The importance of clear requests

One woman told me about a time when she was unhappy that her husband was giving his work too much time and she was feeling neglected and unloved. One night over dinner she commented to him, "You are working far too hard, you need to do fewer hours and take more time off." What she really wanted to say was, "I would like you to work less as I want to spend more time with you." But she was vague, expecting her husband to pick up the hint.

Two weeks later he came home and told her that he had taken on board what she said and booked a two-week golfing holiday with his mates!

Top tip: Agree what important words mean

A top tip is to agree on what important words mean. When Chang says to Kathy (one of his junior managers) that he'd like her to take more ownership of this project, but he doesn't make it clear where the boundaries of ownership sit in his map of the world, he might get a nasty surprise when Kathy makes some unilateral spending decisions that not even he would make without talking to his boss!

3 When by?

"I need it back on my desk in the next two weeks." So how are your anxiety levels on day 13 at 3 p.m. when it's still not on your desk? You could have really benefited from having it at least two days earlier because now you're going to have look at it at the weekend before the Monday morning board meeting. Technically speaking the other person hasn't broken any promises on the two-week delivery time, but you have no idea whether it's going to turn up at all.

Get specific on timings and then ask a clarification question: "Jake, could you just relay back to me what we've agreed on timings?" Once again, check for incongruence in body language or verbal response. If you sense there may be a problem, test your assumption by asking the other person if they have any concerns with the timescales.

4 What might get in the way?

How much depth you go into on this depends on three factors: the other person's competence, how much you trust them and the risk factor in what they are about to do. Encouraging a dialogue about what might stop them from completing the action is a great way to give them a chance to air concerns or bring to your attention stuff that you simply hadn't considered. It's also a useful way of flushing out future excuses if there's been a previous accountability problem.

You may also find it worth discussing at this point when or how either of you should report back regarding any problems that arise and possibly to agree progress checks. This again makes it easier for either party to bring misunderstandings, broken promises or concerns back to the table early on.

5 Walk the talk

Remember, if you have made a commitment, make sure you walk your talk and follow through. If you can't, go back and let the other person know as soon as possible. If you can't stand up and be accountable, why should they?

Summarise and one more check

Finally, simply summarise your understanding of each key aspect or action and then ask one more checking question: "Just so we're absolutely clear, could you let me know what you think we've just agreed?" You will be amazed how many times there are still differences in what each party thinks they have agreed to, even after the 5Ws.

14
Giving Bad News

The focus of this book has been on using a third-generation mindset with the goal of mutual understanding and collaboration. From what you have learned throughout this journey, in most vital conversations you don't have the power to impose a unilateral decision on the other person; or if you did, you wouldn't want to use it. There are times, however, when you have to deliver bad news that is unilateral in nature, whether that's ending a relationship, cancelling a supplier's contract or making someone redundant. In such a scenario, how you deliver the message is crucial.

At the time of writing the world is heading into the most significant global financial crisis since the 1920s. The need to deliver challenging, potentially hurtful or difficult news has never been more acute. And sharing bad news in a recession is not just about losing a job. Cutting back financially may require many vital conversations about budgets, mortgage arrears, spending habits, holidays and lifestyle decisions.

There are certain types of bad news that this chapter does not address, since they are outside the scope of this book. For example, medical teams and other emergency professionals are often required to share bad news with people about severe injury, terminal illness or death.

In addition, it is prudent to point out that when taking any member of staff through a dismissal or disciplinary process, each organisation has its own specific codes of practice. I recommend you contact your HR specialist before you progress with any legalities or formal procedures.

What this chapter does do is examine the emotional impact and consequences of being the deliverer of bad news. It gives you some insights and strategies that will reduce the stress of giving bad news for both you and the recipient.

Real-life case study: A stressful week

Duncan is in his first leadership position in a medium-sized sales organisation. Over the last 18 months he has built a team of 11 sales representatives from scratch and his team consistently performs within the top 5% of those in Europe. He has worked long hours and put a great deal of effort into the team's training. The team members are enthusiastic, hard working, motivated and consequently successful and justly rewarded.

The second week in December, at the European leadership meeting, an announcement is made that due to budget constraints imposed by the US, all European expenditure is to be halved, including the workforce. Half the leaders are told they no longer have a job, the other half are asked to terminate the contracts of half their sales teams.

Fortunately for Duncan he is in the second group. Unfortunately, he has to tell five of his team that they no longer have jobs in the seven working days left before Christmas. The human resource decision criteria are standardised across the organisation and are non-negotiable. Within the five personnel Duncan has to let go are one man in his 30s whose wife is expecting their first child imminently; one is 55 and relocated for the role; one lost his mother the month before. For all five, these are conversations Duncan does not want to have, but he has no choice but to deliver the news in order to keep his own much-needed job.

Many of you may have already have had to impart bad news through no choice of your own. In fact, at times in a leadership role, the corporate decision you have to convey may be against your better judgement, and yet you are selected as the messenger.

Imparting a non-negotiable decision that has life- or career-changing implications has a far greater emotional impact than just at the moment it is announced. While the human brain struggles with change at any level, a life-altering *fait accompli* of the nature described has been shown to closely parallel the psychological impact of the death of a person close to you. You may well both be experiencing a radical shift in their long-term picture of the future and potentially losing what previously felt safe and secure. This will bring on a surge of overwhelming emotion.

The grief cycle

One of the first elements to consider for both the recipient of the news and yourself is that either of you may experience the grief cycle.

Elisabeth Kübler Ross pioneered counselling that helped people handle the personal trauma of death and dying, for both the patients and those in relationships with them. The stages of the grief cycle she developed are:

❖ *Shock*: Initial paralysis at hearing the bad news.
❖ *Denial*: Trying to avoid or ignore the inevitable.
❖ *Anger*: Frustrated outpouring of bottled-up emotion (or guilt if you are giving bad news).
❖ *Bargaining*: Looking in vain for a way out.
❖ *Depression*: Final realisation of the inevitable.
❖ *Testing*: Seeking realistic solutions.
❖ *Acceptance*: Finding a way forward and moving on.

The model has been applied to many other situations less significant than death but still highly traumatic, such as redundancy, enforced relocation, the end of a long-term relationship or bankruptcy.

It's useful to consider this model in relation to both yourself and the person you will be giving the bad news to, as it's likely that you will go through at least one and possibly all of the stages when you deliver the message. You do not necessarily pass through each stage like a product going through stages on an assembly line. In fact, it's more common to get stuck at one stage as you struggle to process the impact of the news and, for the person receiving it, the ramifications for their life as well as for their family members, friends and work colleagues. You can also recycle around a previous stage as you oscillate back and forth between denial, anger and acceptance. In the case of Duncan's organisation, the bad handling and consequent impact of the news breaking even caused many of the remaining workforce to get stuck in a form of guilt known as "survivor syndrome", which led to a significant fall in productivity and employee engagement.

Everyone interprets and handles bad news differently. Some may need silence for a while as they process what has happened, others may react instantly and with passion or anger. Some may be calm and collected at the time, building to an emotional reaction later. Each reaction is valid and worth preparing for, again both from the perspective of the other person and for yourself. The first step in achieving this is to step into the other person's shoes.

Step into their shoes

Take a quiet moment and picture yourself as the person receiving the bad news. How will it affect them, given where they are in their life or career right now? What's the timing of this news like for them? Think of Duncan's team two weeks before Christmas, one about to have their first baby, one having just lost a parent. Would they have seen this coming or would it be a bolt from the blue? How are they going to feel and how do you imagine they will respond?

This process can be emotionally challenging and you may need to call on the skills you have learned throughout this book to allow you to dissect fact from story consciously and clearly.

You may think about your own role in the situation and consider "I should have..." or "I wish I had not..." Those thoughts that sit underneath your analysis can cloud a clear picture of the facts. If you have made a decision or you have been told to impart one, that decision is made. Think now about the other person. Seeing it from their perspective will be useful mental preparation for handling a challenging reaction in a compassionate and productive way; although realise that their response may be completely different in reality.

Be careful to keep your thoughts fact based. The man in his 50s whose contract Duncan had to terminate had left a successful role with a competitor to come and work for him. In his preparation Duncan imagined anger and resentment at being persuaded to move, as well as grief and sorrow at a lost career so late in life and personal disappointment in Duncan as the manager. When it came to having the conversation, this particular person was in fact calm and reflective when he heard the news. He had had a very lucrative and enjoyable year with Duncan and he also felt excitement that this redundancy offer could be just the chance to retire early that he had been looking for.

Being the messenger

Giving bad news can be very tough on the messenger as well as the receiver. Remain ever vigilant about your own story making, since that may rock your emotional and cognitive balance. Inner dialogue that creates untested assumptions about how the other person may judge you – "What will they think of me?" "Will they think I'm a bad person?" – may weaken your ability to deliver the news empathically and clearly, even potentially flipping you into an unnecessarily defensive mindset before you have even started the conversation.

Here are a few further ideas that will help:

❖ Prepare what you are going to say carefully, not necessarily word for word, but know what aspects of the news are not negotiable and what might be flexible. If you know that you absolutely want out of a relationship, then you need to be firm on why you're ending it. If there are consequences regarding logistics, houses, money and possessions, it may be possible to offer joint discussions on those.

❖ Use the emotional state management techniques in this book to prepare mentally. Remember, you can't influence anybody else until you have successfully influenced yourself. You are the person in this conversation who has had time to prepare and plan; the other person has not. Minimise the potential impact on them by remaining focused, compassionate and empathic. Be prepared for what you perceive to be the worst possible outcome and allow yourself to feel confident or at least composed with that.

❖ Knowing the potential impact of breaking bad news, do a final personal mental check that delivering this news is the correct or the only option open to you. If it's the ending of a relationship, have you really explored other paths to saving the relationship and has the other person had a chance to change or talk about the way they see it? If the conversation will achieve your required outcome, know that by thinking it through in detail, you have done your best to make the delivery compassionate, clear and focused.

My aim is that when you are actually giving the bad news, the skills you have picked up in this book will help you to deliver the message and maximise your chances of looking after the other person, the relationship and yourself.

To warn or not to warn?

Duncan's organisation chose to tell people about its financial status the morning after the annual Christmas party; there were no rumours, no warnings. In some employment situations, particularly involving termination of contracts, there is a necessity to give prior warning, often within a series of clear HR processes. This gives the recipient the opportunity to prepare both mentally and legally for the conversation. I am not advocating one correct way of arranging the actual conversation. You need to think through the logistics for the other person as best you can and decide on the basis of each individual situation.

Duncan's team were out on the road, but he knew that the news would spread fast. He rang each affected team member the morning following the announcement and gave them the option of meeting him that day or as soon as they could. Each team member asked what the meeting was for; to some he said he would choose not to discuss the situation over the phone and to some he warned that it was bad news. There was an immediate impact on each of them, and yet Duncan preferred this approach to the out-of-the-blue career shock he and his colleagues had faced the previous day.

Venue and time

Choose the meeting location carefully. You want it to be free of interruptions and in a place that will be conducive to the other person's potential need to release emotion. They may also want to be left alone or not want to be seen leaving. Consider the time carefully. Will rumours have spread? When is the office or home least busy?

My advice is to find a private location, with refreshment and toilet facilities on hand, where there is space for either of you to be alone if required.

Delivering the news

Just because you are delivering a unilateral decision, it does not mean that the conversation has to be a one-way dialogue. The aim is obviously not to get into an extensive debate over why you're wrong about ending the relationship or why the person thinks they should not be fired, but there is plenty of scope for understanding and empathy. This section contains some useful insights into the conversation itself.

Avoid easing in and becoming inhuman

Because you may find it challenging to be seen as a bad person when delivering a bad message, my experience is that people tend to fall back into two habitual strategies when doing so.

When he first called to arrange to meet the father-to-be he had to fire, Duncan spent five minutes on the phone making polite conversation, asking about his wife, his day and how the pregnancy was going before mentioning that he needed to meet him. When the rep asked what the meeting was for, Duncan replied, "Nothing to worry about, no need to worry your wife. I'll tell you everything when I see you." When he shared his approach to this phone call with me at a workshop several years after the redundancies occurred, he explained that he was so afraid of the rep's reaction that he avoided mentioning in any way that bad news needed to be conveyed. Nevertheless, when the experienced sales rep sensed that all was not well and pressed Duncan for more information, it caused far greater upset and anger when Duncan revealed in a very roundabout and unclear way that he had lost his job.

Although this example is extreme, what would it be like if you were on the end of this kind of conversational opener:

"Hi Mike, great to see you. You're looking well. How are things going? You doing OK? Er, umm, I've been asked to speak with you today, because well, this credit crunch fiasco, it's really biting all of us, and the company just isn't doing nearly as well as it was two years ago. Profits are way down, especially the loss of the XYZ contract, that really stuffed things up. Well, I don't really know how to put this, but the decision's been made, it was out of my hands you see. I'm really sorry, I know this is going to be a bit of a shock, I did go out to bat for you but they just wouldn't listen. I can't believe we've reached this point, trust me if there was anything I could do..."

It's clear that the manager is not taking responsibility or ownership for the delivery of the message and the recipient is caused further unnecessary stress, confusion and uncertainty. This easing-in strategy is often used in the misguided belief that it reduces the pain, but in reality it has the opposite effect.

The other extreme form of bad news delivery is one that many managers adopt to handle the rough ride it can lead to. One of my workshop delegates, Jill, shared how as a manager she mentally entered a personality state she named "the bitch". She explained that if she became numb to both her and the other person's emotions, it was easier to stay rational and focused. From this completely detached state it was simple to justify to herself that she was just doing her job, that the decision was good for the business, and therefore that casualties were necessary. Unfortunately for Jill, her approach solidified her reputation as a bitch and in her words she became a managerial leper for whom nobody wanted to work.

Are you likely to employ either of these tactics to ease the pain? Think who the easing in or the inhuman approach are for. Are the words you are using clear and compassionate, or there to ease a guilty conscience?

An example of blending compassion with a clear, concise message is:

"Mike, I've asked to meet with you because I have some bad news. In line with the run of poor corporate results, the company is going to make you redundant. I can imagine this is terrible news, and this is not a conversation I ever wanted to have with you." (Then empathic silence)

The anxiety of delivering the message often makes the deliverer uncomfortable with the silence that may occur when the receiver goes into shock. If you aren't careful, you may end up rambling on, either with further apologies or justifications and next steps.

Let them process

Think back to the grief cycle. The other person may well be in shock and overwhelmed, in which case give them some space to process and reflect on what they have heard. Don't be too quick to dive in with more data, next steps or questions. You may be uncomfortable with the silence, but it may be just what they need to get back to a more emotionally rational place.

Gently explore where they are at

When your intuition rather than personal anxiety tells you it's time to talk again, begin to inquire tentatively. Choose your own words according to the situation and personality you're dealing with, but here's one possible approach:

"Would you be willing to let me know your thoughts and feelings having received this news?"

If the other person responds in a measured or calm way, I recommend simply listening and mirroring back any key feelings they express. When it feels right you may want to talk about where they go from here, next steps and so on. Keep bearing in mind, however, that they are likely to be in shock and that their ability to listen and especially remember things may be severely impaired.

It may well make sense to end the conversation compassionately and arrange another time to discuss details and next steps, after they have had several hours or days to process the news.

There will be times when the response is not calm or controlled, and there are further suggestions on how to handle this below.

What if they cry?

One of my clients, a female manager in a large organisation, had a terrible fear of tears. She worried that she would either say placating words that were not actually useful or true, or cry herself.

It's natural and healthy to cry and release stress when you are overwhelmed. If the other person does cry, my advice is to use words of empathy without agreeing to anything they have said that is not in line with your non-negotiable outcome or bad news. Ask them if they need some time to collect themselves; it may be appropriate to reconvene later so that they have time to process the news.

What if they shout?

Usually, anger is stage two of the grief cycle. If the other person gets angry, the first question you need to ask yourself is whether your physical safety is at risk. If you believe it is, I would close down the conversation as fast as possible and exit the room to a safe place. If you believe that the other person can overcome their neanderthal ancestry and not thump you, then stay and remember that they may not necessarily be angry at you.

Handling the situation is very similar to the approach when you get a strong emotional reaction at the start of a vital conversation:

1. Breathe into your diaphragm and see the human being whose emotion has been triggered by tough news.
2. Let them vent and acknowledge their feelings.

3. Restate the bad news if it sounds like they have rejected or mis-interpreted it.

4. You may also need to use the "and" strategy. For example: "I hear that you are devastated, *and* that you think we still have a future together, *and* that I might regret this down the line, *and* I still know that I will not be happy in this relationship *and* as difficult as this is for me and you to discuss, I still want to end my relationship with you."

The "and" strategy enables you to demonstrate that you have genuinely heard the other person's pain and point of view, while allowing you to remain true to your decision and needs.

Just because you are being unilateral in the end message and outcome does not mean that you cannot explore what is going on for the other person in relation to the outcome. You don't have to agree, but you can still show a lot of understanding. It is also worth remembering that these are rarely one-off conversations and therefore within a few hours or days you may be talking about the next stage. How you handle the first conversation, however, sets the tone and emotional climate for the rest.

Find a caring decompression chamber

Do not underestimate the toll that this kind of conversation can have on your energy, nerves and sanity. Even with the best preparation you can often leave the conversation emotionally drained, upset for both you and the receiver of the bad news.

If it doesn't break confidentiality, find someone you can download to, deconstruct any stories you have built up, and release any self-judgements or emotions you have brought from the conversation. Ask to be heard, not for feedback or opinion at that stage, purely an ear and understanding so that you can allow the conversation to rest.

If you cannot share it, then go for a walk, ideally in nature, to let go of the stress and physical tension that may have built up, write down how you are feeling or use music to help release your emotions. Hold compassion for yourself and know that by using the processes outlined in this chapter, you have handled the worst in the best way you can for both the recipient and yourself.

Afterword

Talking about the things that matter most can be a truly daunting task. My hope is that this book has given you the confidence to realise that your impossible conversation might actually be possible. Unfortunately, I can give you no guarantees that your vital conversation will be the success that you need it to be, and even if you reach a great outcome, the conversational journey that got you there will in all likelihood have been very challenging.

But what is the alternative? We can send a man into space and doctors can perform keyhole surgery on the brain, yet hundreds if not thousands of people are needlessly injured, killed or murdered each day because people fail to resolve their differences through words and instead use deadly force. I see around me a nation of people who are increasingly unhappy with the decisions that politicians, governments and big business are making, and yet our increasing docility and self-imposed helplessness mean that we don't speak up with passion, responsibility and clarity against the hypocrisy, greed and lack of personal accountability that have become so prevalent in the running of our country and its finances.

So what can be done? To quote Mahatma Gandhi, "Let us be the change we want to see in the world." Perhaps if we start with the vital conversations we need to have in our homes, relationships and places of work, we might not only inspire ourselves to talk about what matters most, we just might become role models for others, illuminating a different path that moves society away from both the shackles of silence and the emotional wake created by aggression, manipulation and unilateral control.

I would ask you to have compassion for yourself on the journey of your vital conversations. Using the approach and the skills outlined in the book is a process and not a destination. Only yesterday a series of events that had a negative impact on me sent me careering into a first-generation mindset. I was proud neither of the conversation I had nor the results that the quality of my communication manifested. The reality is that we are all going to have bad days where our best does not get to show up, but that should not stop us from admitting our mistakes and trying to do things better next time.

Although this book has focused on how to plan for big conversations, my hope is that many of you will have worked out that the third-generation approach and the accompanying skills can be applied to all conversations. My recommendation is to bring the essence of this book into all of your communication by eating the elephant one bite at a time. Each day become conscious of one of the skills (e.g. testing assumptions) or key concepts (e.g. letting go of blame) and set an intention to bring that learning to life in the dialogue you have with others. Over several months and probably years with this approach you will see a gradual and yet ever-increasing beneficial change in the quality of your communication, relationships and wider life.

I wish you well with what I see as a life's work.

Vital Conversations Coaching Tool

In combination with the book, this coaching tool will enable you to do some invaluable preparation for your vital conversation. If you would prefer to download a pdf of this coaching tool, go to www.alecgrimsley.co.uk/coachingtool and enter the pass code mentoringtool1.

Be guided by the book in how you use the coaching tool. At various points in the book, key concepts will be explained and then you will be directed back to this coaching tool where you can apply the learning to your particular conversation.

Please note: Using the coaching tool for the first time without using the book as your guide will not only vastly reduce the quality of your preparation, but in all likelihood will lead to a poor outcome in your vital conversation.

If you find there is a question that you're not sure about or it does not seem to relate to your conversation, I would either recommend going back to that particular section of the book for some further clarification, or simply leave the question or box blank and return to it later to see if it becomes applicable as you progress further into the book.

Before using the coaching tool please ensure that you have read Chapter 3 and completed the questions on page 35. Having done this, start with question 1 and then simply read the book and be guided back to this coaching tool when you see the VC coaching tool icon.

Vital Conversations Coaching Tool

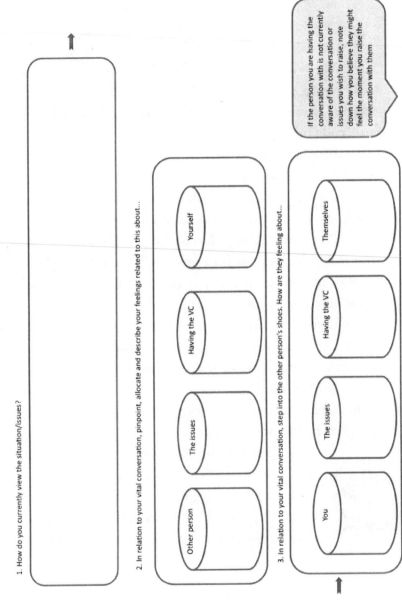

1. How do you currently view the situation/issues?

2. In relation to your vital conversation, pinpoint, allocate and describe your feelings related to this about...

Other person | The issues | Having the VC | Yourself

3. In relation to your vital conversation, step into the other person's shoes. How are they feeling about...

You | The issues | Having the VC | Themselves

If the person you are having the conversation with is not currently aware of the conversation or issues you wish to raise, note down how you believe they might feel the moment you raise the conversation with them

4. Are there any of my core psychological needs that have not been met ? (See page 85 for a more comprehensive list)

5. Up to now, what has been my story about the other person, the issues and my role in this?

5b. What are the actual facts/data (bottom of ladder)?

Vital Conversations Coaching Tool

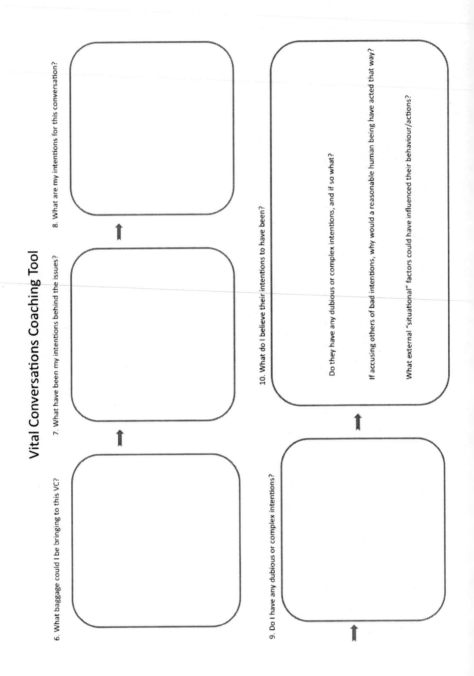

6. What baggage could I be bringing to this VC?

7. What have been my intentions behind the issues?

8. What are my intentions for this conversation?

9. Do I have any dubious or complex intentions?

10. What do I believe their intentions to have been?

Do they have any dubious or complex intentions, and if so what?

If accusing others of bad intentions, why would a reasonable human being have acted that way?

What external "situational" factors could have influenced their behaviour/actions?

Vital Conversations Coaching Tool

Take a systemic view

11. What inputs have contributed to the issue/s?

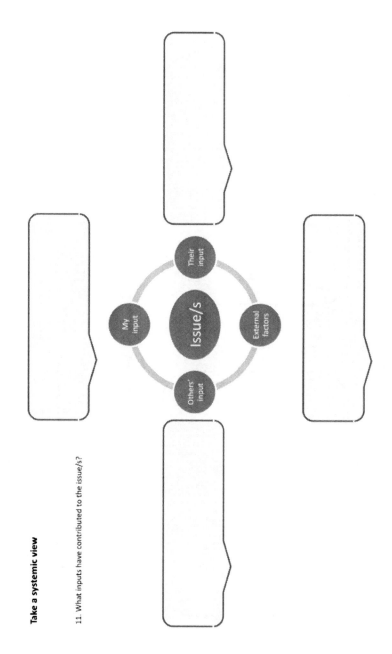

Vital Conversations Coaching Tool

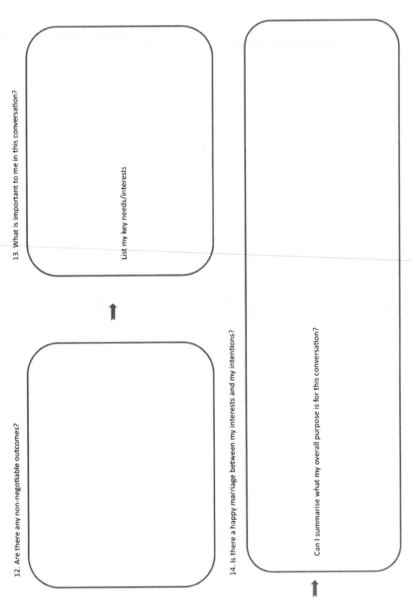

13. What is important to me in this conversation?

List my key needs/interests

12. Are there any non-negotiable outcomes?

14. Is there a happy marriage between my interests and my intentions?

Can I summarise what my overall purpose is for this conversation?

Vital Conversations Coaching Tool

15. How will you start your vital conversation ?

Guidelines for creating your opening statement

1. Keep it under 90 seconds
2. Define the issue and your purpose for having the conversation
3. Express what you believe to be at stake and any consequential impacts
4. If appropriate, include how you feel about this issue and potentially the conversation
5. Express your motivation to find a positive way forward
6. Create the beginnings of a collaborative role for the other person by inviting them to respond
7. Wherever possible, look for ways to codesign how you discuss the issues

Index

Resolution to picture puzzle from page 156.

About the Author

Over the last eight years, through extensive research and practical experience in the field of difficult conversations, Alec Grimsley has cultivated an approach that will enable you to raise and discuss sensitive issues, whether that is in the boardroom, managing difficult people or when giving bad news, such as redundancy or ending a personal relationship.

Alec has run workshops and facilitated leadership teams within organisations including SAP, Thomson Directories, Harrods, AstraZeneca, Nokia, British Airways, NatWest, HSBC, BT, NTL, IBM, Reuters, Norwich Union, Scottish Re, Grant Thornton, Ernst & Young, Deutsche Bank, NHS Trusts, John Lewis, Harvey Nichols, Clear Channel, Disney, Yellow Pages, Asics, Expedia, The White Company and Pearl Assurance.

He is a recognised affiliate of the Association of Business Psychologists and a member of the Professional Mediators Association. He also is a volunteer community mediator for Dorset Mediation, a trust that offers conflict resolution and mediation services for those who would not normally have the financial resources to access such expertise.

Alec is married with two sons and a black Labrador called Wilson. He and his family live on the coast near Poole, Dorset.

Vital Conversations Workshop

Would you like the opportunity to attend the Vital Conversations workshop delivered personally by Alec Grimsley? There is a limit to how much you can learn and integrate from reading a book, so this two-day workshop offers you the opportunity to learn and discuss key concepts with the author as well as undertaking carefully guided role plays and coaching.

As part of the workshop process, Alec will ask you to bring along a vital conversation that you need to have in either your personal or professional life. Throughout the two days he will help you to prepare and build your confidence and capability in having this crucial conversation.

Over the two days you will learn how to:

✔ Get clear on the vital conversations that will make the biggest difference in your team, projects and personal relationships
✔ When to raise an issue and when to let it go
✔ Manage your emotions and confidence throughout a conversation
✔ Convey what's important to you without dancing around the issue
✔ Handle another person's strong emotions
✔ Respectfully question to get beyond others' defensive positions
✔ Go beyond hearing to listening for facts, feelings and needs
✔ Investigate both sides of the "story" to generate real understanding
✔ Maintain a safe and respectful dialogue for discussing tough topics
✔ Understand the mental shift from blame to seeing both parties' inputs
✔ Develop a collaborative approach that generates more options
✔ Say no and still remain in rapport
✔ Gain clarity and joint commitment to mutually agreed next steps
✔ Name the issue and start your conversation with confidence
✔ Plan and successfully execute difficult yet vital conversations
✔ Handle an impromptu difficult conversation

Go to Alec's website at alecgrimsley.co.uk for more information about public and corporate workshops or contact his PA Gerry Hyde on 07917 101657 or email Gerry.hyde@vitalgb.com.

Lightning Source UK Ltd.
Milton Keynes UK

172088UK00001B/4/P